1 Introduction

We estimate a dynamic model of investment and finance to understand and quantify the effects of equity mispricing on these policies. This inquiry is of interest in light of stock market volatility that often dwarfs the volatility of real activity (Shiller 1981). For example, the stock market crash of 2008 was followed by a complete rebound over the subsequent two years, and the technology boom in the late 1990s was followed by a marked reversal in the early 2000s. During these periods, although real activity moved in the same direction, the magnitudes were much smaller. The existence of such wide fluctuations in equity values relative to real activity raises the question of whether these swings reflect movements in intrinsic firm values, or even time-varying expected returns. If not, then it is natural to wonder whether such movements in equity values affect managerial decisions. Put simply, does market timing occur, and how large are its effects?

As surveyed in Baker and Wurgler (2012), many studies have tackled the question of the effects of equity misvaluation and investor sentiment. However, the literature lacks investigations of the quantitative importance of market timing. This type of study is interesting in that economists naturally wish to measure the relative costs and benefits of managerial actions. We fill in this gap by using the estimates obtained from a dynamic model to quantify the effects of market timing on various firm policies. Structural estimation is particularly useful in this situation because misvaluation is, by nature, unobservable. Our model allows us to deal with this challenge by putting enough plausible structure on the data for us to back out the effects of misvaluation.

Our dynamic model captures decisions about a firm's dividends, investment, net cash (cash net of debt), equity issuances, and repurchases. Its backbone is a neoclassical model of physical and financial capital accumulation with profitability shocks, constant returns to scale, costs of adjusting the capital stock, and underwriting costs in the equity and debt markets. The model then incorporates a new feature that is motivated by the behavioral finance literature. Possibly persistent misvaluation shocks separate the market value of equity and its true value, and managers exploit this misvaluation to benefit a controlling block of shareholders at the expense of other shareholders who trade with the firm.

Misvaluation affects the firm because it attenuates the extent to which equity issuances and repurchases cause dilution and concentration of the controlling shareholders' stake. In response to misvaluation, firms predictably repurchase shares when equity is underpriced and issue shares when equity is overpriced. Model parameters then dictate the size of these equity transactions, as well as the size of the misvaluation shocks themselves. They also dictate whether the funds required for repurchases or received from issuances flow out of or into capital expenditures or net cash balances. Quantifying the relative magnitudes of these different effects therefore requires estimating the model's parameters. We use simulated method of moments (SMM), which minimizes model errors by matching model generated moments to real-data moments. We obtain estimates of parameters describing the firm's technology, equity market frictions, and most importantly, the variance and persistence of misvaluation shocks.

We find that our model does a remarkably good job fitting many features of our data, given its simplicity. This good fit is evident not only in large heterogeneous samples of firms, but in homogeneous samples from different industries. Further, we obtain significant estimates of the variance and serial correlation of misvaluation shocks, which are stronger in industries a priori more likely to be subject to equity misvaluation. In short, we find that the model credibly captures those features of the data we wish to understand and shows that misvaluation shocks are important.

Next, we compute impulse response functions, which measure the responses of various policies to a one standard deviation profit shock or misvaluation shock. We find that equity repurchases and issuances respond more strongly to misvaluation shocks than they do to profit shocks, but that these reactions are short lived. In contrast, we find that the strong response of net cash balances to the misvaluation shock is persistent. Finally, we find that investment responds much more strongly to profit shocks than to misvaluation shocks.

Thus, our parameter estimates imply that although firms issue equity when it is overvalued, they only use a small fraction of the proceeds for capital investment. Instead, they tend for the most part to hoard the proceeds as cash or to pay down debt. This saving then gives the firm more flexibility to repurchase shares when equity is undervalued or to respond to profit shocks by investing in capital goods. We conclude that although equity misvaluation appears important for financial policies, its impact on real policies is much smaller.

One advantage of structural estimation is that we can conduct counterfactual exercises, which extend the insights from the impulse response functions by considering hypothetical situations in which the magnitude of misvaluation shocks is different from that implied by our estimates. In particular, we compare a firm, as estimated, with a hypothetical firm that does not experience misvaluation shocks but that is otherwise identical. We find that average equity issuances and repurchases increase sharply with the variance of the misvaluation shocks. In addition, net cash balances also rise strongly. Interestingly, investment also rises with the variance of misvaluation shocks. With no misvaluation, investment is below the level predicted by a model with no financial constraints and then rises slightly above this level. In other words, misvaluation shocks help alleviate financial constraints. Finally, we find that equity market timing in our model increases controlling shareholder value by up to 8%, relative to a model with no misvaluation shocks.

Our paper falls into several literatures. The first is the structural estimation of dynamic models in corporate finance, such as Hennessy and Whited (2005, 2007), DeAngelo, DeAngelo, and Whited (2011), and Morellec, Nikolov, and Schürhoff (2012). These papers examine such issues as capital structure, financial constraints, and agency problems. Our paper is distinctive in that we ask whether behavioral factors affect firm decisions.

Our paper belongs in the large empirical behavioral literature on the effects of market misvaluation on firm policies. For example, Graham and Harvey (2001) find survey evidence that managers explicitly consider the possibility of equity overvaluation when deciding whether to issue shares. Eckbo, Masulis, and Norli (2007) and Baker and Wurgler (2012) provide excellent surveys of the empirical research that tests the more general proposition that market timing is important for many firm decisions. More recently, Jenter, Lewellen, and Warner (2011) find managerial timing ability by examining firms' sales of put options on their own stock, and Alti and Sulaeman (2011) find that high equity returns induce issuances only when there is institutional demand. Our results add to this research by providing the first quantitative evaluation of the effects of misvaluation.

The papers most closely related to ours are Bolton, Chen, and Wang (2013), Eisfeldt and Muir (2012), Yang (2013), and Alti and Tetlock (2013). The first two papers use models related to ours. However, neither quantifies any effects of misvaluation. Instead, Bolton et al. (2013) considers the directional implications of market timing and the comparative statics of risk management. Eisfeldt and Muir (2012) focuses on the role of stochastic issuance costs in explaining the correlation structure among aggregate firm policies, particularly the high correlation between cash saving and external finance. Yang (2013) examines the theoretical effects on capital structure of mispricing that arises from differences in beliefs. Our goal, in contrast, is not to understand where mispricing comes from, but to quantify its effects empirically. Alti and Tetlock (2013) performs a structural estimation of a neoclassical investment model augmented to account for behavioral biases. However, they focus on asset pricing effects of these biases.

The paper is organized as follows. Section 2 describes our data and presents descriptive evidence. Sections 3 and 4 present the model and discuss its optimal policies. Section 5 outlines the estimation and describes our identification strategy. Section 6 presents the estimation results. Section 7 presents our counterfactuals, and Section 8 concludes. The Appendix contains proofs.

2 Data and Summary Statistics

Our data are from the 2011 Compustat files. We remove all regulated utilities (SIC 4900-4999), financial firms (SIC 6000-6999), and quasi-governmental and non-profit firms (SIC 9000-9999). Observations with missing values for the SIC code, total assets, the gross capital stock, market value, or net cash are also excluded from the final sample. The final sample is an annual panel data set with 55,726 observations from 1987 to 2010. We use this specific time period for two reasons. First, prior to the early 1980s, firms rarely repurchased shares, so these data are unlikely to help us understand repurchases. Second, because our model contains a constant corporate tax rate, we need to examine time periods in which tax policy is stable. Therefore, we start the sample after the 1986 tax reforms, because during this period, there is only one major change in tax policy: the Jobs and Growth Tax Relief Reconciliation Act of 2003. Therefore, for some of our estimations, we consider two sample periods, before and after this legislation.

We define our variables as follows. The most difficult is equity issuances because the Compustat variable SSTK contains a great deal of employee stock option exercises. McKeon (2013) shows that these passive issuances are large relative to SEOs and private placements. To isolate active equity issuance, we follow McKeon (2013) and classify management initiated issuances as the amount of SSTK that exceeds 12% of market equity (PRCC_F× CSHO). McKeon (2013) shows that this scheme is highly accurate. Measuring repurchases also requires the consideration of option exercise activity because, as summarized in Skinner (2008), firms usually repurchase shares in order to offset the dilution effects of option exercise. We therefore measure repurchases as PRSTK minus the amount of equity issuance classified as passive. The rest of the variable definitions are standard. Total assets is AT; the capital stock is GPPE; investment is capital expenditures (CAPX) minus sales of capital goods (SPPE); cash and equivalents are CHE; operating income is OIBDP; dividends are the sum of common and preferred dividends (DVC + DVP); debt is (DLTT + DLC); and Tobin's q is the ratio of (AT + PRCC_F× CSHO − TXDB − CEQ) to AT. All other variables are also expressed as fractions of total assets.

We summarize these data in Figures 1 and 2, which plot several variables for small and large firms, respectively. We define a firm as large in a particular year if its assets exceed the median for the sample in that year. Otherwise, we define a firm as small. Panel A in Figures 1 and 2 plots equity issuance, equity repurchases, and dividends, each of which is scaled by total book assets. They also plot the average annual real ex-dividend return on equity. Panel B of each figure contains analogous plots for average debt issuance and saving, each of which is scaled by total assets, and the latter of which is defined as the change in (gross) cash balances. Panel C of each figure contains analogous plots for investment scaled by assets.

We find several patterns of interest. In Panel A of both Figures 1 and 2, we confirm the well-known stylized fact that equity returns and equity issuance track one another fairly closely, especially in the mid-1990s and the late 2000s. This pattern is much more pronounced for small firms than for large firms. We also see that repurchases appear to be slightly negatively correlated with returns. This pattern holds for both large and small firms. Finally, for both groups of firms, dividends are much smoother and decline over the sample period.

In Panel B of Figures 1 and 2, the most striking result is the strong positive comovement between saving and equity returns, especially for the small firms. Interestingly, we find almost no visible relationship between debt issuance and returns for the small firms, and perhaps a slightly negative relationship for the large firms. These results clearly indicate that any relationship between *net* cash changes and returns comes from the cash side rather than from the debt side. Finally, Panel C of these two figures shows that investment in physical assets is much smoother than equity returns and is, if anything, slightly negatively correlated with returns.

We have not interpreted these results because correlations between equity returns and corporate policies might or might not indicate market timing. Market timing is important if equity values contain a component unrelated to fundamental firm value and if managers react to this misvaluation component. In this case, the high correlations between equity transactions and returns are clearly consistent with timing. Further, if timing is indeed occurring, then the high positive correlation between saving and returns suggests that the funds for equity transactions flow in and out of cash stocks. Of course, if equity is not misvalued or if managers do not pay any attention to misvaluation, these high correlations could also simply be a result of managers' attempts to fund profitable investment projects, which are naturally correlated with intrinsic firm value. To disentangle these competing explanations, we therefore estimate a dynamic model.

3 Model

As a basis for our estimation, we use a model that captures a firm's dividend, investment, cash (net of debt), and equity issuance/repurchase decisions. The backbone of this model is a dynamic investment model with financing frictions (e.g. Gomes 2001; Hennessy and Whited 2005). However, it deviates from this basic framework in three important ways. First, it contains a much richer specification of the payout process. Second, we introduce an agency problem in which managers only maximize the value of a subset of shareholders. This second component paves the road for our third addition to the model, which is a deviation of the market value of equity from its true value.

3.1 Cash Flows

We consider an infinitely lived firm in discrete time. At each period, t, the firm's risk-neutral manager chooses how much to invest in capital goods and how to finance these purchases. The firm has a constant returns to scale production technology, $z_t K_t$, that uses only capital, K_t, and that is subject to a profitability shock, z_t. The shock follows an $AR(1)$ in logs:

$$\ln(z_{t+1}) = \mu + \rho_z \ln(z_t) + \varepsilon_{z\,t+1}, \qquad (1)$$

in which μ is the drift of z_t, ρ_z the autocorrelation coefficient, and $\varepsilon_{z\,t+1}$ is an i.i.d., random variable with a normal distribution. It has a mean of 0 and a variance of σ_z.

Firm investment in physical capital is defined as:

$$I_t = K_{t+1} - (1-\delta) K_t, \qquad (2)$$

in which δ is the depreciation rate of capital. When the firm invests, it incurs adjustment costs, which can be thought of as profits lost as a result of the process of investment. These adjustment costs are convex in the rate of investment, and are given by

$$A(I_t, K_t) \equiv \frac{\lambda I_t^2}{2K_t}. \qquad (3)$$

The parameter λ determines the curvature of the adjustment cost function.

If the firm were to maximize its expected present value, given the model ingredients thus far, we would have a neoclassical q model of the sort in Hayashi (1982) or Abel and Eberly (1994). In this type of model, external financing is implicitly frictionless. Thus, we will refer to this benchmark case as the "frictionless" case.

The model we study expands upon this frictionless case in two dimensions. The first is financing. We assume that the firm finances its investment activities by retaining its earnings, issuing debt, and issuing equity. When the firm retains earnings, it holds them as one-period bonds, C_t, that earn the risk-free rate, r. We allow C_t to take both positive and negative values, with the latter indicating that the firm has net debt on its balance sheet. In the model, debt is collateralized by the capital stock, so that the firm faces a constraint

$$-C_t \leq K_t. \qquad (4)$$

Thus, debt is risk-free and the interest rate on debt is r. Because we allow $C_t < 0$, we refer to C_t as net cash. Although debt is risk-free, it incurs proportional issuance costs of the form

$$\Phi(C_{t+1}, C_t) \equiv \phi \operatorname{abs}(\max(C_{t+1} - C_t, C_{t+1})) \mathcal{I}(C_{t+1} < 0, C_{t+1} < C_t),$$

where $\mathcal{I}$ is an indicator function. This formulation implies that changing cash holdings in either direction or reducing debt is costless but that increasing debt is costly.

We denote equity issuances by E_t, with a negative number indicating repurchases. When the firm issues equity, it pays a fixed cost, $a_0 K_t$, which is independent of the size of the issuance, and which can be thought of as an intermediation cost for a seasoned offering. Note that the cost is proportional to the capital stock, which preserves homotheticity in the model.

The firm's profits are taxed at a rate τ_c, with the tax bill, T_t, given by

$$T_t = (z_t K_t - \delta K_t + C_t r)\tau_c. \tag{5}$$

Note that the tax schedule is linear, so that the tax bill can be negative. This simplifying feature captures tax carryforwards and carrybacks. The final financing option available to the firm is adjustment of its dividends, D_t, which are given by a standard sources and uses of funds identity:

$$D_t = z_t K_t - I_t - \frac{\lambda I_t^2}{2 K_t} + C_t(1+r) - C_{t+1} - T_t + E_t - a_0 K_t \mathcal{I}(E_t > 0) - \Phi(C_{t+1}, C_t), \tag{6}$$

in which cash flow net of taxes and equity issuance or repurchases equals the total dividend payout. Finally, we assume that dividends are taxed at a rate τ_d. This assumption implies that in the model as specified thus far, the firm strictly prefers repurchasing shares to paying dividends.

3.2 Agency Problem

As this point the model is a standard neoclassical model of investment with exogenous financing frictions. Although our ultimate goal is to study equity misvaluation and market timing, we first need to consider the inherent agency problem associated with market timing. For a manager to take advantage of misvalued equity, he needs to issue shares when equity is overvalued and repurchase shares when it is undervalued. These transactions transfer wealth from the shareholders who trade with the firm to those who do not. As such, market timing by managers implies that managers do not maximize the value for all shareholders at all times.

To formalize this agency problem, we assume that managers maximize the value for a block of shares that constitute a controlling position of the firm. This controlling block has a fixed number of shares. We do not need to specify the exact size of this block, nor do we impose the restriction that the size of the block remain the same across firms. We do require that the block not constitute all shareholders, and we thus assume that cumulated equity transactions never cause the number of non-controlling shares to go to zero. The block must also be large enough to control the firm. Because the size of a controlling block can be much smaller than 50% (La Porta, Lopez-de Silanes, and Shleifer 1999), we do not need to assume a strict lower bound on the block size.[1] Thus, there are always shareholders available to take the opposite side of the equity transactions that benefit the shareholders in the controlling block. One final detail is that we do not need to require the identity of the shareholders in the controlling block to remain constant; they can sell the shares to new shareholders, who then take over the controlling stake.

We now show how these assumptions affect the managers' maximization problem: first in the case of no misvaluation, and, second, in the case of misvaluation. In both cases, the fraction of total shares outstanding owned by the controlling shareholders varies over time as the firm issues and repurchases shares. We denote this fraction by f_t. In the case of no misvaluation, the value of the controlling block of shares can be written as follows:

$$V^c(f_0, K_0, C_0, z_0) = \max_{\{K_t, C_t, E_t\}_{t=1}^\infty} \mathbb{E}_0 \left(\sum_{t=0}^\infty \beta^t f_t (1-\tau_d) D_t \right). \tag{7}$$

The operator $\mathbb{E}_t$ is the expectation operator with respect to the distribution of z_t, conditional on the information at time 0. As we assume that the controlling block does not engage in equity transactions with the firm, its value does not incorporate payouts from repurchases.

We assume that the value of the controlling block is linear in the fraction of shares it owns:

$$V^c(f_t, K_t, C_t, z_t) = V(K_t, C_t, z_t) f_t. \tag{8}$$

This assumption reflects the fact that an increase in the fraction of shares in the block translates into an increase in the fraction of dividends received by the block shareholders. The linearity assumption requires that the fraction not have any influence on the dividend policies of the firm.

Under this assumption, we can rewrite the value of the controlling block as:

$$V(K_0, C_0, z_0) = \max_{\{K_t, C_t, E_t\}_{t=1}^\infty} \left\{ (1-\tau_d) D_0 + \mathbb{E}_0 \left(\sum_{t=1}^\infty \beta^t \frac{f_t}{f_0} (1-\tau_d) D_t \right) \right\}, \tag{9}$$

---

[1] Although imposing restrictions on the size of the controlling block renders the model intractable, for all of our sets of estimated parameters, block size relative to firm size rarely shrinks. Also, in 1,000 simulations, if the block starts at 50%, it always takes longer than 100 simulated years to increase or decrease by 40 percentage points.

where the initial dividend payment has been pulled out of the summation. The infinite sum (9) can be expressed in recursive form as the Bellman equation:

$$V(K,C,z) = \max_{K',C',E} \left\{ (1-\tau_d)D + \beta \mathbb{E}\left(\frac{f'}{f}V(K',C',z')\right) \right\}, \tag{10}$$

where a prime indicates a variable tomorrow and no prime indicates a variable today. Thus, we have translated the problem of maximizing the value of the block shareholders into a problem of maximizing the total dividend payment of the firm, while taking into account the evolution of the fraction of shares owned by the block.

The next proposition shows that it is possible to express f'/f solely in terms of the current state variables, (K,C,z), and thus eliminate it from (10).

Proposition 1 *The solution to the Bellman equation in (10) is the same as the solution to:*

$$V(K,C,z) = \max_{K',C',E} \left\{ (1-\tau_d)D + \beta \frac{V(K,C,z) - D}{V(K,C,z) - D + E} \mathbb{E}\left(V(K',C',z')\right) \right\}. \tag{11}$$

The relevant constraints for (11) are the capital stock accumulation identity (2), the definition of dividends in (6), the collateral constraint in (4), and the following nonnegativity constraints:

$$K' \geq 0, \qquad D \geq 0.$$

As in Bazdresch (2013), (11) is isomorphic to a standard Bellman equation without the dilution/concentration term $(V(K,C,z) - D)/(V(K,C,z) - D + E)$. However, we now show that this isomorphism needs to be modified when equity is misvalued.

3.3 Misvaluation

The next model ingredient is a misvaluation shock, ψ, that determines the ex-dividend equity value, V^*, at which equity transactions occur. In particular, V^* is a stochastic multiple of the ex-dividend target equity value that the managers maximize for the controlling block. We denote this target value as $V(K,C,\psi,z)$, so that we can write V^* as:

$$V^* = (V(K,C,\psi,z) - D)\psi. \tag{12}$$

Note that $V(K,C,\psi,z)$ differs from the fundamental value of the firm that would be obtained in the absence of misvaluation. This difference arises because managers actively optimize the value of the controlling block in response to misvaluation shocks. Thus, we call $V(K, C, \psi, z)$ "target value" because it is a function of the misvaluation term, ψ.

The misvaluation shock, ψ, follows the first-order autoregressive process:

$$\ln \psi' = \mu_\psi + \rho_{z\psi} \ln z + \rho_\psi \ln \psi + \varepsilon'_\psi, \tag{13}$$

where, ρ_ψ is the serial correlation of the shock, and ε_ψ is a normally distributed *i.i.d.* shock with mean zero and variance σ_ψ. It is uncorrelated with the shock to the profitability process, ε_z. Nonetheless, this specification allows for correlation between the misvaluation and profitability processes. This correlation occurs through the $\rho_{z\psi}$ term, which implies that the current profitability level impacts the conditional expectation of the future misvaluation level. This model feature is motivated by the notion that investors over-extrapolate, so overvaluation is more likely to occur during good times, while undervaluation is more likely to occur during bad times. The μ_ψ term is set such that the unconditional expectation of the misvaluation term equals 1. This calculation is detailed in the Appendix. When $\psi = 1$, the firm is valued correctly; when $\psi < 1$, the firm is undervalued; and when $\psi > 1$, the firm is overvalued.

Several different models can rationalize the presence of market mispricing. The first is simple asymmetric information, where the manager can observe the shock; that is, he knows the target value of the firm and can therefore observe deviations of target from market values. However, market participants cannot observe target value. If misvaluation stems solely from asymmetric information between the manager and outsiders, then for it to be persistent, there must exist frictions that prevent market participants from eventually inferring target firm value. An example of such a friction might be exogenous incomplete markets, as in Eisfeldt (2004), or a continuous inflow of private information. Another plausible theory of misvaluation is Scheinkman and Xiong (2003), which does not rely on asymmetric information. Instead, market participants disagree about target value, and short-sale constraints imply that optimal trading strategies result in mispricing. Another plausible theory is in Hellwig, Albagli, and Tsyvinski (2009), where traders receive heterogeneous signals about firm value, and the market price imperfectly aggregates these signals.

Although motivated by these various theories, our shock is exogenous to the firm's decisions, which implies that managers do not manipulate market expectations about firm value. Nonetheless, our specification of an exogenous shock allows us to model investment and a rich set of financing options in a dynamic setting. These features of our model are essential for quantifying the effects of mispricing on the firm.

In our model, misvaluation affects the quantity of shares that the firm must issue to obtain a given amount of financing, which impacts the evolution of the fraction of shares owned by the controlling block, f. The next proposition formally incorporates this idea into the Bellman equation.

Proposition 2 *In the presence of misvaluation, the Bellman equation for the value function being optimized by the controlling block is:*

$$V(K, C, \psi, z) = \max_{K', C', E} \left\{ (1 - \tau_d)D + \beta \frac{V(K, C, \psi, z) - D}{V(K, C, \psi, z) - D + E + \frac{E}{\psi}} \mathbb{E}\left(V(K', C', \psi, z')\right) \right\}. \quad (14)$$

The operator $\mathbb{E}$ is now the expectations operator with respect to the joint distribution of z and ψ, conditional on the information today.

Proposition 2 shows that under the assumption that the manager optimizes the value of a controlling block of shareholders, the manager's problem in the presence of misvaluation can be translated into a Bellman equation that diverges from the standard problem only in rate at which the fraction of shares held by the controlling block evolves over time. As such, despite the nonstandard specification of (14), it is fully time consistent under the assumption that the equity transactions occur with shareholders that are not part of the controlling block.

Finally, we note that our agency-based framework for modeling managerial decision making in the presence of misvaluation is quite general. It can be applied to dynamic models with different technological and financing assumptions, and even different state variables.

3.4 Price Impact

If misvaluation occurs because of asymmetric information between market participants and the firm, market participants are likely to infer from the firm's equity repurchase and issuance decisions that the share price may be overvalued or undervalued and then bid the price down or up. See, for example, the evidence in Brockman and Chung (2001). Further, even in the absence of asymmetric information or misvaluation, there can be a price impact for large trades if some traders face capacity or margin constraints, as in Gârleanu and Pedersen (2011) or He and Krishnamurthy (2013). We model this phenomenon in a reduced-form way by assuming that the price of equity transactions is inversely proportional to $1 + \nu(E, K)$, where:

$$\nu(E, K) \equiv \frac{1}{2}\left(\nu_i\left(\frac{E}{K}\right)\mathcal{I}(E > 0) + \nu_r\left(\frac{E}{K}\right)\mathcal{I}(E \leq 0)\right), \qquad \nu_i, \nu_r \geq 0. \tag{15}$$

Note that $\nu(E, K)$ is a function of the fraction E/K. This assumption maintains homotheticity in the model and embodies the notion that the price impact of an equity transaction depends on the size of transaction relative to firm size. This piecewise linear specification implies that for a given equity issuance, $E > 0$, the firm must issue more shares to offset the price impact as $\nu(E, K) > 0$. It also implies that for a given repurchase, $E < 0$, the firm can retire a smaller number of shares than it would be able to in the absence of the price impact, as $\nu(E, K) < 0$. Price impact therefore affects the evolution of the fraction of shares owned by the controlling block. The reduced-form specification of (15) implies that if asymmetric information is the force behind the price reaction, informational frictions prevent traders from completely inferring the firm manager's target valuation, $V(K, C, z, \psi)$.[2]

The Bellman equation in the presence of price impact is thus given by the following proposition.

Proposition 3 *If equity transactions induce a price impact according to (15), then the Bellman equation for maximizing the value of the controlling block is:*

$$V(K, C, \psi, z) = \max_{K', C', E}\left\{(1 - \tau_d)D + \beta \frac{(V - D)\psi}{(V - D)\psi + E(1 + \nu(E, K))} \mathbb{E}\left(V\left(K', C', \psi', z'\right)\right)\right\}. \tag{16}$$

One important implication of our motivation for the price impact term is the form the model takes in the absence of misvaluation. If price impact can occur outside of misvaluation, then by setting $\psi = 1$ in (16), we obtain a standard neoclassical model with financing frictions.

It is not obvious that a solution to (16) exists, inasmuch as the discount factor need not always be less than one. However, as in Bazdresch (2013), the following proposition allows the Bellman equation (16) to be written with a constant discount factor.

---

[2] For tractability, we must also assume that the price impact for equity trades does not affect the process for ψ in (13). Because our estimates of price impact do not imply a large effect on the dilution or concentration of blockholder value, this assumption likely has little impact on our results.

Proposition 4 *The solution to (16) is identical to the solution of*

$$V(K,C,\psi,z) = \max_{K',C',E} \left\{ (1-\tau_d)D - \frac{E(1+\nu(E,K))}{\psi} + \beta \mathbb{E}\left(V\left(K',C',\psi',z'\right)\right) \right\}. \quad (17)$$

It is straightforward to show that (17) satisfies the conditions in Stokey and Lucas (1989) that are necessary for the existence and uniqueness of a solution.

It is important to note that the Bellman equation (17) does not imply that the model contains stochastic issuance costs, as in Bolton et al. (2013) or Eisfeldt and Muir (2012). This distinction is important for three reasons. First, the misvaluation shock directly affects the price of equity capital and thus affects *both* repurchases and issuances, instead of just issuance. Second, our model has the potential to generate realistic covariances between equity values and firm policies, whereas models with stochastic issuance costs cannot because they do not generate sufficient equity variability. Finally, the misvaluation shock has no direct impact on the budget constraint (6) that defines dividends, whereas stochastic issuance costs would.

Our model is, nonetheless, closely related to those in Bolton et al. (2013) or Eisfeldt and Muir (2012). Like the model in Bolton et al. (2013), our model contains homogeneous production and financing technologies, fixed cost of equity issuance, cash, and short-term debt. One key difference is that our model contains serially correlated shocks, whereas the model in Bolton et al. (2013) has *i.i.d.* shocks.[3] Although the model in Bolton et al. (2013) is cast in continuous time, and the model in Eisfeldt and Muir (2012) is cast in discrete time, our model is closer to the former than the latter. In contrast to our model, the model in Eisfeldt and Muir (2012) contains a decreasing returns technology, no debt, and both fixed and quadratic costs of adjusting the capital stock.[4] Their model also contains an aggregate productivity shock. Our model is unique with respect to both of these models not only in the modeling of the misvaluation shocks discussed above, but also in the distinction in our model between dividends and repurchases.

3.5 Constant Returns to Scale Specification

Our model can be further simplified by taking advantage of its constant returns to scale nature, and redefining all of the quantities in the model as a fraction of the capital stock, K. Define the

---
[3]The closely related model in Bolton, Chen, and Wang (2011) also contains these basic features.
[4]The estimate of a fixed cost of adjustment in our model is small and insignificant; so we have left it out.

following scaled variables:

$$c \equiv \frac{C}{K}, d \equiv \frac{D}{K}, e \equiv \frac{E}{K}, i \equiv \frac{I}{K}, v(c, \psi, z) \equiv \frac{V(K, C, \psi, z)}{K}.$$

Then, by dividing all of the variables in (17) by K, we obtain the following Bellman equation:

$$v(c, \psi, z) = \max_{c', e, i} \left\{ (1 - \tau_d) d - \frac{e(1 + \nu(e, 1))}{\psi} + \beta \mathbb{E} \left(v\left(c', \psi', z'\right) (1 - \delta + i) \right) \right\}, \tag{18}$$

and the constraints become:

$$d - e + \mathcal{I}(e > 0) a_0 = z(1 - \tau_c) - i - \frac{\lambda i^2}{2} + c(1 + r - r\tau_c) - c'(1 - \delta + i) + \delta \tau_c - \Phi(c, c'), \tag{19}$$

$$d \geq 0 \tag{20}$$

$$-c \leq 1.$$

4 Optimal Policies

In this section, we analyze the first-order conditions for optimal financial and investment policies.

Equity and Dividends

We start with equity and dividend policy, holding optimal investment and net cash policy fixed. The right-hand side of (19) is then also fixed. Let e^* be the unconstrained best equity policy, which is the optimal policy absent the constraint (20). We solve for e^* by substituting (19) into (18), differentiating with respect to e, and setting the result equal to zero. We also must ensure that e^* is large enough to warrant paying this cost; that is, the payoff to equity holders if the firm issues equity must exceed the payoff when it does not. Unconstrained optimal equity policy is given by:

$$e^* = \begin{cases} (\psi(1 - \tau_d) - 1)/\nu_i > 0 & \text{for } \psi > 1/(1 - \tau_d) \text{ and } (e^* - a_0)(1 - \tau_d) - e^*(1 + \nu_i e^*/2)/\psi < 0 \\ (\psi(1 - \tau_d) - 1)/\nu_r < 0 & \text{for } \psi < 1/(1 - \tau_d) \\ 0 & \text{otherwise}, \end{cases} \tag{21}$$

where the last expression on the first line of (21) is the extra optimality constraint that arises from the fixed cost. This constraint implies an inaction region in which the firm neither issues nor repurchases shares. Outside this region, for ψ sufficiently large, the firm wishes to issue equity, and for ψ sufficiently small, the firm wishes to repurchase shares. The higher the parameters ν_i and ν_r, the smaller the desired issuance and repurchasing activity. The dividend tax implies that when

$\psi = 1$, the optimal policy in the absence of the constraint (19) is to repurchase shares. If equity policy is given by (21), desired dividends then are given by (19).

Of course, these first-order conditions ignore the constraint (20), which provides an important link between the real and financial sides of the firm. If the first-order conditions in (21) produce optimal dividends that are positive, then (21) holds exactly. However, if (21) implies that optimal dividends are negative, the constraint binds, so that they are zero. Optimal equity issuance is then given not by (21) but by the budget constraint (19). The policy implied by the budget constraint always trumps the policy implied by the first-order condition when the the two policies differ. Thus, mispricing is not the sole determinant of equity policy: funding needs matter as well.

Table 1 contains a schematic that categorizes the possible combinations of optimal equity and dividend policies. For brevity, we denote the right-hand side of the budget constraint (19) as b. Then we have $d - e + \mathcal{I}(e > 0)a_0 = b$.

Table 1: Optimal Equity and Dividend Policies

case	first-order condition	budget constraint	equity policy	dividend policy
(1)	$e^* < 0$	$b > -e^*$	$e = e^*$	$d = b + e > 0$
(2)	$e^* < 0$	$0 < b < -e^*$	$e = -b$	$d = 0$
(3)	$e^* < 0$	$b < 0$	$e = -b + a_0 > 0$	$d = 0$
(4)	$e^* > 0$	$b > 0$	$e = e^*$	$d = b + e - a_0 > 0$
(5)	$e^* > 0$	$-e^* - a_0 < b < 0$	$e = e^*$	$d = b + e - a_0 > 0$
(6)	$e^* > 0$	$b < -e^* - a_0$	$e = -b + a_0 > 0$	$d = 0$
(7)	$e^* = 0$	$b > 0$	$e = e^* = 0$	$d = b > 0$
(8)	$e^* = 0$	$b < 0$	$e = -b + a_0 > 0$	$d = 0$

The second column of Table 1 describes the equity policy given by (21) alone, that is, e^*. The third column lists various possibilities for the value of the budget constraint, b, relative to 0 and to e^*. The fourth and fifth columns list the optimal equity and dividend policies, respectively.

Cases (1)–(3) are those in which the firm would repurchase shares if it had no budget constraint. Each case corresponds to a different situation vis-à-vis the budget constraint. In Case (1), the firm has ample resources after implementing its optimal investment and cash policies, so it simultaneously pays dividends and repurchases shares. This situation can occur because the tax disadvantage of cash implies that the firm will not optimally want to retain all of its earnings after it exhausts profitable investment projects. Case (1) is also interesting because it shows that the model can allow for simultaneous dividends and repurchases. To the extent that price impact can occur even in the absence of misvaluation, this case demonstrates that misvaluation is not required for simultaneous dividends and repurchases. Second, in Case (2), the firm has enough resources to repurchase shares, but not enough to attain the level given by e^*. Dividends are thus zero. Third, if the firm requires external equity funding ($b < 0$), as in Case (3), then it issues equity, even though equity is undervalued. Misvaluation in this case makes equity issuance extremely costly. Not only does the firm have to pay the issuance cost, a_0, but it is forced by the budget constraint to float shares in a state of the world in which it would be optimal to repurchase shares.

The next three cases describe overvaluation. If the right-hand side of (19) is positive, as in Case (4), the firm issues equity, and then uses the proceeds, plus b to pay dividends. If, as in Case (5), $b < 0$ but this deficit is more than filled by the level of equity issuance given by e^*, then once again, the firm both issues equity and pays dividends. If the firm is both overvalued and requires a great deal of external equity finance, as in Case (6), then the firm issues equity but pays no dividends.

Cases (7) and (8) concern the inaction region in which $e^* = 0$. In this region, the firm never repurchases shares. If $b > 0$, then the firm pays dividends and engages in no equity transactions. On the other hand, if $b < 0$, the firm issues equity to fill the funding gap and then pays zero dividends.

Investment

We now turn to the first-order condition for optimal investment, which we obtain by differentiating (18) with respect to i:

$$(1 - \tau_d + \gamma)(1 + \lambda i) = \beta \mathbb{E}\left(v\left(c', \psi', z'\right)\right). \tag{22}$$

Here, γ is the Lagrange multiplier on the dividend nonnegativity constraint (20). Naturally, this first-order condition appears similar to that from a neoclassical q model. If the dividend nonnegativity constraint does not bind, then the marginal cost of investment is $(1 + \lambda i)(1 - \tau_d)$. At an optimum, this marginal cost equals the discounted expected value of $v(c', \psi', z')$, which is the target value of the firm divided by the capital stock. Financing frictions add an additional component to the marginal cost of investment, which is the Lagrange multiplier term γ. This term implies that investment is more costly to the firm in those states of the world in which more investment would force the dividend nonnegativity constraint to bind. Conversely, if overvaluation induces a large equity issuance, then the dividend nonnegativity constraint is less likely to bind, and the firm will likely invest more. This latter effect confirms the common intuition that overvaluation relaxes financial constraints by making equity financing cheap.

Examining the marginal benefit of investment, given by the right-hand side of (22), also reveals useful intuition. If there is no misvaluation ($\psi = 1$), and if net cash is zero, then the right-hand side of (22) equals the expected value of Tobin's q, which we define as $\psi v(c, z, \psi) - c$. Thus, misvaluation has no *direct* effect on the marginal benefit of investment, but it does have an *indirect* effect because it affects the target value that managers maximize for the controlling block. Thus, both over- and undervaluation can affect investment policy via this channel.

Net Cash

Let $\mathcal{I}_c$ be an indicator function that is one when the firm is issuing debt. We obtain the first-order condition for net cash by differentiating (18) with respect to c':

$$(1 - \delta + i - \phi \mathcal{I}_c) = \beta \mathbb{E}\left(v_c(c', \psi', z')(1 - \delta + i)\right). \tag{23}$$

Next we use the envelope condition to eliminate $v_c(c', \psi', z')$ from the problem. Let ξ be the Lagrange multiplier associated with the collateral constraint (4). Substituting in the envelope condition and rearranging gives:

$$(1 - \delta + i - \phi \mathcal{I}_c) = \beta \mathbb{E}\left((1 + r - r\tau_c + \phi \mathcal{I}'_c)(1 + \gamma' + \xi')(1 - \delta + i)\right). \tag{24}$$

To interpret (24), we first set $\phi = 0$, so that the $(1 - \delta + i)$ terms cancel. The right-hand side of (24) is the expected discounted value of cash, which is simply the after tax principal and interest on net cash balances. The Lagrange multipliers γ' and ξ' then that net cash is more valuable when the dividend constraint or the collateral constraint is expected to bind. In particular, the Lagrange multiplier ξ' means that the firm avoids bumping up against the collateral constraint. Net cash (equivalently, debt capacity) thus has value because it confers financial flexibility. This intuition is standard in investment models augmented for financing (e.g. Gamba and Triantis 2008). In our model with misvaluation, this motive for holding net cash implies that the firm sometimes finds it optimal to issue equity even when it has not hit its debt capacity. If $\phi \neq 0$, then (24) shows that there is an inaction region for debt issuance. As in the case of investment, misvaluation has both direct and indirect effects on optimal net cash policy. Misvaluation indirectly alters (24) through its effect on target firm value, $v(c, z, \psi)$. The direct effect of misvaluation occurs through the Lagrange multiplier γ'.

Numerical Policy Functions

In Figure 3, we plot the policy functions for investment, net cash, issuances/repurchases, and dividends, which we denote as $\{c', i, e, d\} = h(c, \psi, z)$. We parameterize the model using the first estimates reported subsequently in Table 2.[5]

Panel A of Figure 3 depicts the optimal choices of net cash, investment, equity issuances/repurchases, and dividends as a function of the misvaluation shock. The x-axis contains possible values of the shock. It has a log scale because the shock is approximately lognormally distributed. A value of 1 indicates no misvaluation. To construct this panel, we have fixed the profit shock and the current-period level of net cash at their respective sample means from a model simulation.

As expected, given the first-order conditions in (21), Panel A shows that the equity policy function slopes upward, with an inaction region in the center that stems from the fixed issuance cost. Outside of this inaction region, undervaluation results in repurchases, and overvaluation results in issuance. More interesting is the contrast between the policy functions for investment and net cash. The former is largely flat, except for a slight upward slope when the firm is issuing equity. In contrast, the policy function for net cash largely tracks the policy function for equity issuance. This contrast occurs because our parameter estimates indicate that investment is more costly to adjust than net cash. Thus, the firm uses debt financing for repurchases and hoards the proceeds from issuances as cash. Finally, the policy function for dividends is also flat, except for a slight uptick for extreme overvaluation. This pattern can also be understood in terms of Cases (4) and (5) in Table 1, in which desired equity issuance is so high that there are proceeds left over to

---
[5]Policy functions calculated with parameters from our other estimations are qualitatively similar.

distribute to shareholders after all other optimal policies have been funded.

Panel B Figure 3 depicts the response of investment, net cash, issuances/repurchases, and dividends to the profitability shock, z. For this panel, we fix the level of ψ at $1/(1-\tau_d)$ and the current-period level of net cash at the sample mean from a model simulation. In contrast to the result in the Panel A, investment responds strongly and positively to the profitability shock because the profitability shock is the one-period marginal product of capital. The response of optimal net cash to the profitability shock is nonmonotonic. For most of the range of z, net cash increases slightly. When z rises, the increase in the marginal product of capital implies that the firm substitutes physical assets for financial assets. However, there is also an positive income effect on net cash from a higher z, because costly external finance confers a flexibility benefit on net cash. The income effect dominates for most of the range of z. For extremely high levels of z, the flexibility benefit of higher net cash is negligible because the firm is flush with resources. Thus, the firm increases net debt (decreases net cash) to finance capital accumulation.

Equity transactions do not vary with the profitability shock, remaining at 0 over the entire range of z. When $\psi = 1 < 1/(1-\tau_d)$, (21) shows that zero equity transactions are optimal unless the firm's optimal cash and investment policies, together with the budget constraint (19), indicate that the firm needs external equity financing. However, for the level of current cash underlying Figure 3, the firm never optimally needs to fund investment with equity issuance. In contrast, dividends do respond to the profitability shock, but only when it is high. In these states of the world, the firm has more than enough internal funds to finance its optimal investment program, so it pays the residual out to shareholders.

The main conclusions to be drawn from Figure 3 are as follows. First, investment is mostly affected by shocks to profitability and not by equity market misvaluation. Second, net cash policy is affected by both profitability and misvaluation shocks. Finally, equity issuance policy is affected far more by misvaluation shocks than by profitability shocks. It is worth noting that these patterns are in no way hardwired into the model because different arbitrary parameters can yield policy functions with different shapes. For this reason, we analyze the model only for the parameter values that we *estimate*, so that the results are empirically relevant.

5 Estimation and Identification

In this section, we first explain how we estimate the parameters of the model from Section 3. We then discuss our identification strategy.

5.1 Estimation

We estimate most of the structural parameters of the model using simulated method of moments (SMM). However, we estimate some model parameters separately. For example, we estimate the risk-free interest rate, r, as the average real 3-month Treasury bill rate over the sample period of interest. We set the corporate tax rate equal to 20%. This level is lower than the statutory rate because we omit personal taxes on interest from the model. Finally, we set the tax rate on dividends, τ_d equal to the difference between the statutory rates on dividends and capital gains.

We then estimate the following 12 parameters using SMM: the fixed equity issuance cost, a_0; the linear debt issuance cost, ϕ; the drift, standard deviation, and autocorrelation of the profitability process, μ, σ_z and ρ_z; the quadratic adjustment cost parameter, λ; the standard deviation and autocorrelation of the misvaluation process, σ_ψ and ρ_ψ; the market-timing penalties, ν_i and ν_r, the correlation between the misvaluation and profitability shocks, $\rho_{z\psi}$, and the depreciation rate, δ.

Although computationally cumbersome, SMM is conceptually simple. First, we generate a panel of simulated data using the numerical solution to the model. Specifically, we take a random draw from the distribution of $\left(\varepsilon'_z, \varepsilon'_\psi\right)$, conditional on $(\varepsilon_z, \varepsilon_\psi)$, and then compute $v(c, \psi, z)$, $(c', e, i) = h(c, \psi, z)$, and various functions of $v(c, \psi, z)$, c', e, and i, such as Tobin's q. We continue drawing values of $\left(\varepsilon'_z, \varepsilon'_\psi\right)$ and using these computations to generate an artificial panel of firms. Next, we calculate interesting moments using both these simulated data and actual data. SMM then picks the model parameters that make the actual and simulated moments as close to each other as possible. The Appendix provides details.

One important issue for estimation is unobserved heterogeneity in our data from Compustat. These firms differ along a variety of dimensions, such as technology and access to external finance. In contrast, the only source of heterogeneity in our model is the individual draws of $(\varepsilon_z, \varepsilon_\psi)$. Therefore, we remove the heterogeneity from the actual data, using fixed firm effects in the estimation of variances and covariances. We calculate autocorrelation coefficients using the method in Han and Phillips (2010), which controls for heterogeneity at the firm level.

This issue of heterogeneity implies that SMM estimates the parameters of an average firm, not the average of the parameters across firms. These two quantities are not the same because the model is nonlinear. Because it is often difficult to conceptualize an average firm in a large population of firms over a long time span, we first examine subsamples of firms that are homogeneous along the time and size dimensions, as in Figures 1 and 2 We examine separately the time periods before and after the Jobs and Growth Tax Relief Reconciliation Act of 2003. Within these two time periods, we then analyze small and large firms, so that we end up with four groups of firms.

5.2 Identification

The success of this procedure relies on model identification, which requires that we choose moments that vary when the structural parameters vary. In making these choices, we do not want to "cherry-pick" moments because we want to understand what features of the data our model can and cannot reconcile. Therefore, we examine the mean, standard deviation, and serial correlation of all of the variables we can compute from our model: investment, profits, equity issuances, equity repurchases, net cash, equity returns, and Tobin's q. We construct our simulated variables as follows. Net cash is c, investment is i, net saving is $c'(1 - \delta + i) - c$, equity issuance is $\max(e, 0)$, repurchases are $\min(-e, 0)$, and returns are $(\psi'v')/(\psi v) - 1$.

We now describe and rationalize the 19 moments that we match. Of particular interest is finding moments that can be used to identify the standard deviation and serial correlation of the misvaluation shock, ρ_ψ and σ_ψ, as well as the correlation between the two shocks, $\rho_{z\psi}$. Because both the misvaluation shocks and profitability shocks affect firm policies, this task is difficult.

Of great help in this endeavor are the mean, standard deviation, and serial correlation of operating profits, which are defined in the model as z. The only model parameters that induce any variation in these three moments are the drift, residual standard deviation, and serial correlation of the profitability shock, μ, σ_z, and ρ_z. Therefore, these three parameters can be pinned down using only these three moments. Roughly speaking, with these three parameters pinned down, moments related to the market value of the firm can be used to pin down ρ_ψ, σ_ψ, and $\rho_{z\psi}$.

We use five moments related to market values. The first four are the standard deviation and serial correlation of Tobin's q and equity returns.[6] All four moments are useful for identifying the standard deviation and the serial correlation of the misvaluation process, σ_ψ and ρ_ψ. Intuitively, the standard deviations of returns and Tobin's q are strongly increasing in σ_ψ. The serial correlation of Tobin's q increases with ρ_ψ, while the serial correlation of returns decreases with ρ_ψ because returns are roughly the first difference of Tobin's q, which is stationary in the model. The fifth moment we use to identify misvaluation shocks is the slope coefficient from regressing equity issuance on returns, which is generally increasing in $\rho_{z\psi}$. Issuance is determined by both ψ and z, and so is firm value, so the higher the correlation between ψ and z, the more issuance covaries with returns.

Our next moments are the mean, serial correlation, and standard deviation of the rate of investment, i. The standard deviation is useful for identifying the adjustment cost parameter, λ, because higher λ produces less volatile investment. The serial correlation is primarily affected by the smooth adjustment cost parameter, as well by the serial correlation of the profitability process, ρ_z. The mean of investment is particularly useful for identifying the depreciation rate of capital, as average investment is strongly increasing in this parameter.

The rest of the moments pertain to the firm's financing decisions. We include the mean, serial correlation, and standard deviation of the ratio of net cash to assets. The standard deviation of net cash decreases sharply with ϕ and is thus useful for its identification. We also include the mean and standard deviation of the ratio of equity issuance to capital, the incidence of equity issuance, and the mean and standard deviation of the ratio of repurchases to capital. These moments are useful for identifying the equity issuance cost parameter, a_0, the parameters penalizing equity transactions, ν_i and ν_r. The incidence of issuance is particularly useful for identifying the standard deviation of the misvaluation shock. Absent the misvaluation shock, the model can produce lumpy, infrequent issuance that is used to fund investment. However, the frequency is much smaller than what is in the data. The presence of the misvaluation shock helps bridge this gap.[7]

---

[6] We omit the means of Tobin's q and equity returns because our model cannot capture rents to capital or the equity premium, which largely determine the means of these two variables, respectively.

[7] We omit moments related to dividends. As is the case with all investment-based models of financing (e.g. Hennessy and Whited 2005, 2007), the model-implied variance of dividends far exceeds the smoothness observed

6 Results

This section presents estimates of the model from Section 3, as well as from an identical model that we augment to contain time-varying expected returns. We also report estimations from different industries.

6.1 Baseline Estimation

Panel A of Table 2 shows that the model fits the data surprisingly well. Across the four estimations, approximately half of the simulated moments are statistically significantly different from their data counterparts,[8] but only a handful are *economically* different. This good fit is remarkable, given that we have used many more moments than parameters in the estimation. The model does a particularly good job of matching the mean and standard deviation of investment and profits, the standard deviations of returns and Tobin's q, the mean, standard deviation, and incidence of equity issuances, and the standard deviation of repurchases. In particular, the model comes close to matching the high net cash of the small firms in the latter part of the sample. Further, the ability of the model to match the standard deviation of profits is important. Otherwise, if the model could not generate sufficient variability in profits, this shortcoming would put substantial weight on misvaluation to generate sufficient variability in firm policies. The model does a fair job of matching the rest of the net cash means, as well as several of the serial correlations. The model struggles with only two features of the data: the standard deviation of net cash and the mean of repurchases. The simulated net cash standard deviation is up to 50% too large, and simulated average repurchases are from 50% to 300 % too large.

Panel B of Table 2 presents the parameter estimates we obtain from each of our four samples. Most of the parameters are statistically significant. Two exceptions are the estimates of the equity issuance cost parameter (a_0) from the late period. This result is not surprising, given the rise of the practice of shelf registration of equity offerings (Gao and Ritter 2011). The other exceptions are three of the estimates of the shock correlation parameter, $\rho_{z\psi}$, and all of the estimates of the

---

in the data. If we use dividend moments in the estimation, this model failure causes many moments to be poorly matched. Therefore, any counterfactuals constructed using the poorly fitting simulated moments produce inaccurate inferences.

[8] In all cases, we also reject the joint hypothesis that all moment conditions are zero.

debt issuance cost parameter, ϕ. The insignificant of ϕ is not surprising, given that the marginal dollar of debt issued often comes from a credit line.

More importantly, for all four samples, the standard deviation and serial correlation of the misvaluation shocks are highly statistically significant. The estimates of the standard deviation range from 0.4 to 0.48, while the estimates of the serial correlation range from 0.73 to 0.82. These estimates seem large at first glance. However, it is important to remember that these figures are for the driving process of $\ln(\psi)$, not the level of ψ. Thus, the standard deviation estimates are roughly comparable to return standard deviations, which for individual companies often exceed 60%. We conclude that a great deal, but by no means all of the variability in market values fails to reflect the manager's view of fundamentals.

The economic magnitudes of many of the other parameters are plausible. For example, the estimates of δ correspond to the average ratio of investment to assets seen in Compustat data, and the adjustment cost parameters correspond to the range of estimates of the coefficient on Tobin's q reported in, for example, Whited (1992). The two parameters that are difficult to interpret are ν_i and ν_r. One way to interpret these parameters is in terms of the amount of issuance it would take in the absence of these parameters to generate the amount of dilution or concentration of the value of the controlling block that occurs, given the estimated values of ν_i and ν_r. These figures are reasonable. For example, according to the early-small estimation, an equity issuance of 1% of firm value has a dilution effect for long-term shareholders equal to an issuance of 1.12% of firm value in a frictionless setting with no ν_i term. These dilution effects range from 1.12% to 1.14% for the other three samples. The figures for repurchases imply that the concentration of the holdings of controlling shareholders ranges from 0.85% to 0.95% for a 1% equity repurchase. In sum, although we find a large amount of perceived misvaluation, these parameter estimates indicate that managers are cautious to respond to them due to potential adverse market responses.

6.2 Pricing Kernel

We now ask whether our estimates of the variance of the misvaluation shock are simply picking up movements in rational expected returns and not misvaluation, per se. To address this concern, we add an aggregate productivity term to our model that is calibrated to match the duration and severity of expansions and recessions in the United States and an associated pricing kernel. See the Appendix for details. Table 3 presents our estimates of this augmented model. The augmented model fits the net cash moments worse than the baseline model, but it fits the repurchase moments better. Interestingly, the point estimates for the standard deviation and serial correlation of the misvaluation shock are lower than in they are in the baseline model. However, these estimates are still significantly different from zero. Thus, our estimates of the misvaluation parameters in Table 2 do pick up some movement in expected returns. However, time-varying expected returns cannot completely account for the levels of the misvaluation shock standard deviation.

6.3 Industry Estimation

The parameter estimates we obtain are for an average firm, not an average parameter across firms. Therefore, we now estimate the model using data from homogeneous groups of firms that are stratified by two-digit SIC industry. This exercise provides a stricter test of the model's ability to rationalize the data from very different types of firms.

Because our highly nonlinear estimations require a great deal of data for identification, we choose the eight two-digit SIC codes with the most data points. SIC13 is oil and gas extraction; SIC20 is food products; SIC28 is chemicals and allied products; SIC35 is machinery and computer equipment; SIC26 is electronic and electrical equipment; SIC38 is measuring instruments; SIC50 is wholesale trade; and SIC73 is business services.

We first present the moment estimates. For brevity, Figure 4 displays our results from matching an important subset of moments: the means of the four policy variables in our model, which are investment, net cash, equity issuances, and repurchases. Each panel in Figure 4 corresponds to a different moment, with the x-axes containing the simulated moments and the y-axes containing the data moments. Each pair of data moment and corresponding simulated moment is then labeled by the relevant industry SIC code.

Panels A and B show that the model does an excellent job of matching average net cash and investment. These moment pairs line up nicely along their respective 45° lines, and only two of these pairs represent significant differences. This result is particularly strong, given the large differences in the moments across industries. For example, oil and gas extraction has high net debt of approximately 20% of assets, while business services has high net cash of approximately 5% of assets. As seen in Panel C, the model does not do as good a job matching average equity issuance, with most industries well matched, but with simulated issuance for oil and gas extraction too low. Panel D shows that the model does a somewhat worse job with average repurchases. Simulated repurchases are too high in three of the eight industries. Nonetheless, the model can capture the broad range of issuances and repurchases seen in the data. In the language of asset pricing, the model captures the "spread" observed in these different moment conditions.

Table 4 contains the parameter estimates. We concentrate on the estimates of the standard deviation and serial correlation of the process for the misvaluation shock. The industries with the lowest variance shocks are SIC20 (food products), SIC50 (wholesale trade), and SIC 13 (oil and gas extraction). The industries with the highest variance shocks are SIC35 (machinery and computer equipment), SIC38 (instruments), and SIC73 (business services). It is useful to compare these estimates with other measures of misvaluation. Unfortunately, the misvaluation of an entire group of firms is hard to gauge. Nonetheless, we find it plausible that firms in high R&D industries are more opaque, and thus more likely to suffer from misvaluation. The bottom row of Table 4 contains average R&D for the firms in each industry. Interestingly, the lowest R&D industries (food and wholesale) also have the lowest variance misvaluation shocks, while the highest R&D industries have the highest. This result thus constitutes a useful external model validation exercise that lends credibility to the interpretation of ψ as a misvaluation shock, as opposed to some other source of variability.

7 Counterfactuals

We now quantify the effects of misvaluation via counterfactual exercises. First, in Figure 5 we measure the change in firm policies when we alter the standard deviation of the misvaluation shock process. To construct this figure, we parameterize the model with the early-large estimates in Table 2.[9] We then solve the model 20 times, each time corresponding to a different value of σ_ψ, with the

---

[9] The results using the other model parameterizations are qualitatively similar.

rest of the parameters held at their estimated values. For each model solution, we simulate 150,000 firm-year observations, and then compute the averages of five variables.

Panel A of Figure 5 plots repurchases and equity issuance as a function of the standard deviation of the misvaluation shock, σ_ψ. In both cases, we average in observations with zero activity. Not surprisingly, average equity issuances and repurchases increase with the misvaluation shock standard deviation. To understand whether the increase in issuance is due to size or frequency, we also plot the incidence of equity issuance. Interestingly, average incidence rises almost parallel with average issuance, which means that the average size of an issuance remains roughly constant. Only the frequency increases with misvaluation shock standard deviation.

In Panel B of Figure 5, we plot average net cash and average investment as a function of σ_ψ. Net cash is much higher for firms that face higher standard deviation misvaluation shocks. Although average investment is also higher, this effect is much more modest. For reference, we also plot the level of investment that would result from a frictionless neoclassical investment model with the same profitability shock process, depreciation rate, and investment adjustment costs. Interestingly, we find that firms overinvest relative to this level, except at the lowest misvaluation shock volatility. This result is interesting because it shows that in the model misvaluation shocks allow firms to issue equity when the existence of equity issuance costs would make this source of financing prohibitively expensive, that is, misvaluation alleviates financial constraints. We find that this effect does not result in the same level of investment that would occur in a frictionless environment. Instead, the resulting level of investment is somewhat higher.

Panel C of Figure 5 plots the average value of the controlling block, v as a function of σ_ψ, where we have normalized the value with no misvaluation to be one so that the plot isolates the value of timing. The effect of σ_ψ is modest, especially for low shock standard deviations. One question we can answer from this plot is how much controlling shareholders' value would be lost if the shock standard deviation were zero instead of its estimated value of 0.43. Equivalently, how much value would be lost if the manager followed the optimal policies of a firm that experienced less (or no) misvaluation, but worked in a firm subject to misvaluation. We find that the controlling shareholders would lose 8.2% of their equity value.[10] This figure is likely an upper bound for the actual amount of lost value. When we change the misvaluation shock standard deviation, we do so holding all other parameters constant. However, it is unlikely that the market response to equity issuance and repurchases (as captured by the parameters ν_i and ν_r) would remain the same in a low misvaluation environment. Indeed, these parameters would likely be somewhat smaller and equity transactions would be less constrained. More liberal equity policies would then attenuate the drop in the value of controlling shareholders' equity.

To understand the economic mechanisms behind this result, we examine the immediate impact of misvaluation shocks by calculating impulse response functions. Once again, we parameterize the model using the estimates from the large firms in the early period. This exercise differs from our comparative statics exercises in which we change a model *parameter* and then examine its impact on average firm policies. Instead, we are looking at the immediate response of a single variable to an actual realization of a shock. Calculating an impulse response function with real data requires estimating, inverting, and orthogonalizing a vector autoregression because the shocks that drive the variables of interest are unobservable. However, in our simulated data we *do* observe our shocks, so to calculate our impulse response functions, we simply regress our variables of interest on each of our two shocks, which we standardize and orthogonalize using a Cholesky decomposition.

The results are in Figure 6. The y-axis in each panel contains the *change* in the variable of interest in response to a one standard deviation shock. The x-axis is time since the shock realization. The most striking result is in Panel A, which depicts net cash balances. A one standard deviation misvaluation shock raises net cash balances by over 3% of assets. This substantial effect dies out only after three years. As shown in Panels B–D, the effects of a one standard deviation misvaluation shock are also noticeable on issuances and repurchases, but to a much lesser extent on investment.

The effects of the profit shock are noticeably different in magnitude. First, a one standard deviation profit shock has a negligible effect on average cash balances. Next, we find that issuance and repurchases respond only weakly to the profit shocks. In the case of issuance, a one standard deviation shock does not induce such a large investment that the firm wishes to pay the fixed

---

[10]The corresponding figures for our other three samples are between 6.1% and 7.9%.

issuance cost to finance the investment with equity. In contrast, profit shocks have a much stronger effect on investment than do misvaluation shocks.

Finally, we conduct an informal "out-of-sample" test of the validity of our model, in the sense that we want to ascertain whether it can reconcile patterns in the data that were not used to estimate it. In particular, given our interest in market timing, we want to ascertain whether our model can replicate the correlations between equity returns and a variety of different variables. Table 5 contains the results from this comparison. We do separate calculations for the four samples from Table 2: early/small, early/large, late/small, and late/large. The actual data correlations are correlations between the aggregate variables depicted in Figures 1 and 2. The simulated correlations are from data simulated from the model, given the four different parameterizations.

For all four samples, we match the signs of the correlations between returns and investment, net saving, equity issuance, and repurchases. For the two early samples, we also match many of the actual magnitudes of the correlations. Our model struggles more with matching the large magnitude of the correlations from the latter part of the sample; however, these magnitudes are primarily driven by the 2007–2009 financial crisis. Our model does not do as good a job at matching the signs of the correlations between returns and dividends, which is not surprising because we have no moments related to dividends in our estimation. Nonetheless, given that we only use one out of these five correlations (returns versus issuance) in our estimation, our ability to replicate other correlations bolsters confidence in the model.

8 Conclusion

In this paper, we quantify the extent to which nonfundamental movements in the price of a firm's stock affect its various policies. Although this topic has been addressed by a large number of studies, we approach the problem in a new way—structural estimation—with the intent of adding quantitative results to this body of literature. We estimate a version of a constant returns neoclassical investment model in which equity financing is costly, the firm can accumulate cash and issue debt, and, most importantly, equity values can be subject to misvaluation shocks. In the model, firms naturally issue equity when it is overvalued and repurchase equity when it is undervalued.

Depending on the model parameters, the funds flowing to and from these activities can come from either changes in (net) cash balances or changes in investment, or both.

We find that non-fundamental movements in equity prices (misvaluation) are large. Our counterfactual exercises show that firms issue and repurchase equity in response to misvaluation shocks, but the proceeds from these issuances and the funds from these repurchases flow into and out of net cash balances. The immediate impact on real investment expenditures is small. This result echoes the descriptive findings in McLean (2011) that firms tend to hoard the proceeds from equity issuances. These higher net cash balances provide firms with more financial flexibility, which in turn adds to the equity value of controlling shareholders. In short, misvaluation has large effects on financial policies, much smaller effects on real investment policies, and modest valuation effects.

One admitted drawback of our approach is our modeling of misvaluation shocks as exogenous. This modeling choice is necessary for tractability, which allows us to examine the interesting question of market timing quantitatively. However, this choice makes it difficult to answer questions related to managers' manipulation of share prices. If managers do attempt to misguide shareholders, then their reactions to mispricing might differ from those produced by our model. Examining this type of framework is an interesting avenue for future research.

References

Abel, Andrew B., and Janice C. Eberly, 1994, A unified model of investment under uncertainty, *American Economic Review* 84, 1369–1384.

Alti, Aydoğan, and Johan Sulaeman, 2011, When do high stock returns trigger equity issues?, *Journal of Financial Economics* 103, 61–87.

Alti, Aydoğan, and Paul Tetlock, 2013, How important is mispricing?, *Journal of Finance*, forthcoming.

Baker, Malcolm, and Jeffrey Wurgler, 2012, Behavioral corporate finance: An updated survey, in George Constantinides, Milton Harris, and Réne Stulz, eds., *Handbook of the Economics of Finance*, volume 2 (Elsevier, North-Holland).

Bazdresch, Santiago, 2013, Financial lumpiness and investment, *Journal of Economic Dynamics and Control*.

Bolton, Patrick, Hui Chen, and Neng Wang, 2011, A unified theory of tobin's q, corporate investment, financing, and risk management, *Journal of Finance* 66, 1545–1578.

Bolton, Patrick, Hui Chen, and Neng Wang, 2013, Market timing, investment, and risk management, *Journal of Financial Economics* 109, 40–62.

Brockman, Paul, and Dennis Y. Chung, 2001, Managerial timing and corporate liquidity: evidence from actual share repurchases, *Journal of Financial Economics* 61, 417–448.

DeAngelo, Harry, Linda DeAngelo, and Toni M. Whited, 2011, Capital structure dynamics and transitory debt, *Journal of Financial Economics* 99, 235–261.

Duffie, Darrell, and Kenneth J Singleton, 1993, Simulated moments estimation of markov models of asset prices, *Econometrica* 61, 929–52.

Eckbo, B. Espen, Ron W. Masulis, and Oyvind Norli, 2007, Security offerings, handbook of corporate finance: Empirical corporate finance, e. eckbo, in B. Espen Eckbo, ed., *Handbook of Corporate Finance: Empirical Corporate Finance* (Elsevier, Amsterdam).

Eisfeldt, Andrea, and Tyler Muir, 2012, Aggregate issuance and savings waves, manuscript, UCLA.

Eisfeldt, Andrea L., 2004, Endogenous liquidity in asset markets, *Journal of Finance* 59, 1–30.

Erickson, Timothy, and Toni M. Whited, 2002, Two-step GMM estimation of the errors-in-variables model using high-order moments, *Econometric Theory* 18, 776–799.

Gamba, Andrea, and Alexander Triantis, 2008, The value of financial flexibility, *Journal of Finance* 63, 2263–2296.

Gao, Xiaohui, and Jay Ritter, 2011, The marketing of seasoned equity offerings, *Journal of Financial Economics* 97, 33–52.

Gârleanu, Nicolae, and Lasse Heje Pedersen, 2011, Margin-based asset pricing and deviations from the law of one price, *Review of Financial Studies* 24, 1980–2022.

Gomes, Joao F., 2001, Financing investment, *American Economic Review* 91, 1263–1285.

Graham, John R., and Campbell R. Harvey, 2001, The theory and practice of corporate finance: Evidence from the field, *Journal of Financial Economics* 60, 187–243.

Han, Chirok, and Peter C. B. Phillips, 2010, GMM estimation for dynamic panels with fixed effects and strong instruments at unity, *Econometric Theory* 26, 119–151.

Hayashi, Fumio, 1982, Tobin's marginal q and average q: A neoclassical interpretation, *Econometrica* 50, 213–224.

He, Zhiguo, and Arvind Krishnamurthy, 2013, Intermediary asset pricing, *American Economic Review* 103, 732–770.

Hellwig, Christian, Elias Albagli, and Aleh Tsyvinski, 2009, Information aggregation and investment decisions, Manuscript, Harvard University.

Hennessy, Christopher A., and Toni M. Whited, 2005, Debt dynamics, *Journal of Finance* 60, 1129–1165.

Hennessy, Christopher A., and Toni M. Whited, 2007, How costly is external financing? Evidence from a structural estimation, *Journal of Finance* 62, 1705–1745.

Ingram, Beth F., and Bong-Soo Lee, 1991, Simulation and estimation of time series models, *Journal of Econometrics* 47, 197–205.

Jenter, Dirk, Katharina Lewellen, and Jerold B. Warner, 2011, Security issue timing: What do managers know, and when do they know it?, *Journal of Finance* 66, 413–443.

La Porta, Rafael, Florencio Lopez-de Silanes, and Andrei Shleifer, 1999, Corporate ownership around the world, *Journal of Finance* 54, 471–517.

McKeon, Stephen, 2013, Firm-initiated versus investor-initiated equity issues, Manuscript, University of Oregon.

McLean, R. David, 2011, Share issuance and cash savings, *Journal of Financial Economics* 99, 693 – 715.

Morellec, Erwan, Boris Nikolov, and Norman Schürhoff, 2012, Corporate governance and capital structure dynamics, *Journal of Finance* 67, 803–848.

Scheinkman, Jose A., and Wei Xiong, 2003, Overconfidence and speculative bubbles, *Journal of Political Economy* 111, 1183–1220.

Shiller, Robert J., 1981, Do stock prices move too much to be justified by subsequent changes in dividends?, *The American Economic Review* 71, 421–436.

Skinner, Douglas J, 2008, The evolving relation between earnings, dividends, and stock repurchases, *Journal of Financial Economics* 87, 582–609.

Stokey, Nancy L., and Robert E. Lucas, 1989, *Recursive Methods in Economic Dynamics* (Harvard University Press, Cambridge, MA).

Whited, Toni M., 1992, Debt, liquidity constraints, and corporate investment: Evidence from panel data, *Journal of Finance* 47, 1425–1460.

Yang, Baozhong, 2013, Capital structure with heterogeneous beliefs and market timing, *Journal of Corporate Finance* .

Appendix

This Appendix contains the proofs of Propositions 1–4, the derivation of μ_ψ, the model that contains time-varying expected returns, and an outline of the estimation procedure.

Proof of Proposition 1

Let Q denote the number of shares outstanding for the firm, and let F denote the number of shares in the controlling block. As noted above, F is a constant. The fraction of shares in the controlling block is then given by $f = \frac{F}{Q}$. The ex-dividend price per share of the firm equals $\frac{V(K,C,z)-D}{Q}$. Consider an equity issuance of E. Such an issuance will involve an increase in the quantity of shares outstanding of $N = \frac{QE}{V(K,C,z)-D}$, which follows from dividing the value of the issuance by the share price. Thus, the quantity of shares outstanding evolves according to the following equation:

$$Q' = Q + \frac{QE}{V(K,C,z) - D}. \tag{A.1}$$

Some algebra reveals:

$$\frac{Q'}{Q} = \frac{V(K,C,z) - D + E}{V(K,C,z) - D}. \tag{A.2}$$

Following the definition of the fraction of shares in the controlling block,

$$\frac{f'}{f} = \frac{Q}{Q'}. \tag{A.3}$$

This expression reflects the fact that an increase in the quantity of shares outstanding will reduce the fractional ownership of the controlling block. Substituting (A.3) into (A.2) and taking the inverse, one obtains:

$$\frac{f'}{f} = \frac{V(K,C,z) - D}{V(K,C,z) - D + E}. \tag{A.4}$$

Thus, the evolution of the fraction of shares held by the controlling block can be written solely in terms of firm value, dividends and equity issuance. Finally, the fraction $\frac{f'}{f}$ can be taken to the other side of the expectations operator in (11) because it is determined solely by current period variables.

Proof of Proposition 2

To demonstrate that the Bellman equation for the model with misvaluation, but without price impact, takes the form of (14), we need to derive the fraction f'/f. We start with the number of shares in an equity transaction, which is:

$$N = \frac{QE}{V^*} = \frac{QE}{\psi(V(K,C,\psi,z) - D)}. \tag{A.5}$$

We now obtain the following expressions for the evolution of the fraction of shares held by the controlling block.

$$\begin{aligned}
Q' &= Q + \frac{QE}{\psi(V(K,C,\psi,z) - D)}, \\
\frac{Q'}{Q} &= \frac{\psi(V(K,C,\psi,z) - D) + E}{\psi(V(K,C,\psi,z) - D)}, \\
\frac{f'}{f} &= \frac{\psi(V(K,C,\psi,z) - D)}{\psi(V(K,C,\psi,z) - D) + E}, \\
\frac{f'}{f} &= \frac{V(K,C,\psi,z) - D}{V(K,C,\psi,z) - D + \frac{E}{\psi}}.
\end{aligned} \tag{A.6}$$

Proof of Proposition 3

As above we need to express the number of shares in a given equity transaction:

$$N = \frac{QE(1 + \nu(E,K))}{V^*(K,C,\psi,z) - D} \tag{A.7}$$

We can now use equation (A.7) and proceed as above to derive the evolution of the fraction of shares held by the controlling block.

$$\begin{aligned}
Q' &= Q + \frac{E(1+\nu(E,K))Q}{\psi(V(K,C,\psi,z) - D)}, \\
\frac{Q'}{Q} &= \frac{\psi(V(K,C,\psi,z) - D) + E(1+\nu(E,K))}{\psi(V(K,C,\psi,z) - D)}, \\
\frac{f'}{f} &= \frac{\psi(V(K,C,\psi,z) - D)}{\psi(V(K,C,\psi,z) - D) + E(1+\nu(E,K))}, \\
\frac{f'}{f} &= \frac{V(K,C,\psi,z) - D}{V(K,C,\psi,z) - D + \frac{E}{\psi}(1+\nu(E,K))}.
\end{aligned}$$

Proof of Proposition 4

Let $\tilde{V}$ be a solution to equation (16), with corresponding policy functions $\tilde{D}$ and $\tilde{E}$. Then one obtains from (16):

$$\tilde{V}(K,C,\psi,z) = \tilde{D} + \beta \frac{\psi(V - \tilde{D}(1-\tau))}{\psi(V - \tilde{D}) + \tilde{E} + \nu(\tilde{E}, K)} \int V(K', C', \psi', z') \, dg\left(\varepsilon'_\psi, \varepsilon'_z, | \varepsilon_\psi, \varepsilon_z\right).$$

Rearranging the dividend term and dividing the numerator and denominator of the left hand side by ψ gives

$$\tilde{V}(K,C,\psi,z) - \tilde{D} = \beta \frac{(V - \tilde{D}(1-\tau))}{(V - \tilde{D}) + \frac{\tilde{E}}{\psi} + \frac{\nu(\tilde{E},K)}{\psi}} \int V(K', C', \psi', z') \, dg\left(\varepsilon'_\psi, \varepsilon'_z, | \varepsilon_\psi, \varepsilon_z\right)). \quad (A.8)$$

Next, divide(A.8) throughout by $\tilde{V}(K,C,\psi,z) - \tilde{D}$ and multiply by $\tilde{V}(K,C,\psi,z) - \tilde{D}(1-\tau) + \tilde{E}/\psi + \nu(\tilde{E}, K)/\psi$ to obtain

$$\tilde{V}(K,C,\psi,z) - \tilde{D} + \frac{\tilde{E}}{\psi} + \frac{\nu(\tilde{E},K)}{\psi} = \beta \int V(K', C', \psi', z') \, dg\left(\varepsilon'_\psi, \varepsilon'_z, | \varepsilon_\psi, \varepsilon_z\right),$$

Thus $\tilde{V}$, $\tilde{D}$, and $\tilde{E}$ also solve equation (17).

Conversely, let $\hat{V}$ be a solution to equation (17), with corresponding policy functions $\hat{D}$ and $\hat{E}$. One can use a similar approach to the above to show that $\hat{V}$, $\hat{D}$, and $\hat{E}$ also solve (16).

Derivation of μ_ψ

Define the following matrices:

$$Y = \begin{bmatrix} \ln z \\ \ln \psi \end{bmatrix}, C = \begin{bmatrix} \mu_z \\ \mu_\psi \end{bmatrix}, R = \begin{bmatrix} \rho_z & 0 \\ \rho_{z\psi} & \rho_\psi \end{bmatrix}, \epsilon = \begin{bmatrix} \epsilon_z \\ \epsilon_\psi \end{bmatrix}, \Sigma = \begin{bmatrix} \sigma_z^2 & 0 \\ 0 & \sigma_\psi^2 \end{bmatrix}.$$

Then, the joint transition equation can be written as the following VAR(1):

$$Y_{t+1} = C + RY_t + \epsilon, \quad \epsilon \sim N(0, \Sigma).$$

The unconditional mean of Y is given by the following expression:

$$E[Y] = (I_2 - R)^{-1} C,$$

where I_n denotes a identity matrix of order n. The unconditional variance of Y is given by:

$$\text{Vec}(\text{Var}(Y)) = [(I_4 - (R \otimes R)]^{-1} \text{Vec}(\Sigma),$$

where Vec denotes the vectorization operator and $\otimes$ denotes the Kronecker product. For notational convenience, let $M = [(I_4 - (R \otimes R)]^{-1}$. One can then derive the unconditional mean and variance of $Y(2) = \ln \psi$ as:

$$E[\ln \psi] = \frac{1}{(1-\rho_z)(1-\rho_\psi)} (\rho_{z\psi}\mu_z + (1-\rho_z)\mu_\psi),$$

$$\text{Var}(\ln \psi) = M(4,1)\sigma_z^2 + \frac{\sigma_\psi^2}{(1-\rho_\psi^2)},$$

where $M(4,1)$ denotes the $(4,1)^{\text{th}}$ element of the matrix M. The restriction that the unconditional expectation of the misvaluation term equals one implies that

$$\ln E[\psi] = 0, \quad \Rightarrow \quad E[\ln \psi] + 0.5 \text{Var}(\ln \psi) = 0.$$

Some algebra then reveals that

$$\mu_\psi = -\left[\frac{1}{2}(1-\rho_\psi)M(4,1)\sigma_z^2 + \frac{\sigma_\psi^2}{2(1+\rho_\psi)} + \frac{\rho_{z\psi}\mu_z}{1-\rho_z}\right].$$

Time-Varying Expected Returns

Let x_t be an aggregate productivity variable that takes one of two values, x_l, x_h. Let x_l denote a recessionary state and x_h an expansionary state ($x_h > x_l$). The probability of remaining in a recessionary state is given by p_l, and the probability of remaining in an expansionary state is given by p_h. This implies expected durations of recessions and expansions of $1/(1-p_l)$ and $1/(1-p_h)$, respectively. In addition, we impose the restriction that the unconditional expectation of the aggregate productivity shocks equals 1 so that average profits remains unchanged from the previous model.[11]

The expected return varies with aggregate productivity x_t. Denote the conditional expected return as

$$\beta m(x, x').$$

Following the production-based asset pricing literature, the time-varying expected return can be parameterized as a function of current and future aggregate productivity. Thus,

$$\ln m(x, x') = m_0 + m_1(x' - x).$$

---
[11]Formally, this imposes the restriction that $x_h \frac{1-p_l}{2-p_h-p_l} + x_l \frac{1-p_h}{2-p_h-p_l} = 1$.

Economic reasoning suggests that investors place a higher valuation on assets that payoff in bad states of the world. This imposes the requirement that $m_1 < 0$. In order to ensure that average discount rates remain unchanged from the model without aggregate shocks, we require that $E[m(x, x')] = 1$.[12]

Given these assumptions, the expanded model can be written as follows:

$$v(c, \psi, z, x) = \max_{c', e, i} \left\{ d(1 - \tau_d) - \frac{e(1 + \nu(e, 1))}{\psi} + \beta \mathbb{E}\left(m(x, x')v(c', \psi', z', x')(1 - \delta + i)\right) \right\}$$

$$d - e + \mathcal{I}(e > 0)a_0 = zx(1 - \tau_c) - i - \frac{\lambda i^2}{2} + c(1 + r - r\tau_c) - c'(1 - \delta + i) + \delta\tau_c\Phi(c, c'),$$

$$-c' \leq \phi, \qquad d \geq 0.$$

The solution to the expanded problem takes into account that the static allocation decisions now depend on the aggregate productivity state. It also takes into account the impact of the pricing kernel $m(x, x')$ and the transition matrix for x on the expected future value of the firm.

We calibrate p_l and p_h to match average durations of recessions and expansions of 16 and 42 months, respectively.[13] We calibrate x_l and x_h to generate an average decline in output from its trend growth path of 4%, similar to the output declines observed in U.S. post-war recessions. Combined with the restriction that $E[x] = 1$, one obtains $x_h = 1.011$ and $x_l = 0.971$. This calibration leads to a spread between expected returns in the high and low states of 1.54%.

Estimation

We now give a brief outline of the estimation procedure, which draws from Ingram and Lee (1991) Duffie and Singleton (1993), but which is adapted to our panel setting. Suppose we have J variables contained in the data vector x_{it}, $i = 1, \ldots, n$; $t = 1, \ldots, T$. We assume that the $J \times T$ matrix x_i is i.i.d., but we allow for possible dependence among the elements of x_i. Let $y_{itk}(b)$ be a data vector from simulation k, $i = 1, \ldots, n$, $t = 1, \ldots, T$, and $k = 1, \ldots, K$. Here, K is the number of times the model is simulated. (In practice, K is the simulated sample size, 150,000, divided by the actual

---

[12]This yields the following equation:

$$\exp(m_0)\left[\frac{1 - p_h}{2 - p_h - p_l}(p_l + (1 - p_l)\exp(m_1(x_h - x_l))) + \frac{1 - p_l}{2 - p_h - p_l}(p_h + (1 - p_h)\exp(m_1(x_l - x_h)))\right] = 1.$$

[13]See http://www.nber.org/cycles.html for information on the duration of recessions.

sample size).

The simulated data, $y_{itk}(b)$, depend on a vector of structural parameters, b. In our application $b \equiv (\alpha_1, \lambda, \delta, \rho_\psi, \sigma_\psi, \mu, \rho_z, \sigma_z, \nu_i, \nu_r, \rho_{z\psi})$. The goal is to estimate b by matching a set of simulated moments, denoted as $h(y_{itk}(b))$, with the corresponding set of actual data moments, denoted as $h(x_{it})$. Our moments are listed in the text, and we denote the number of moments as H. Define the sample moment vector:

$$g(x_{it}, b) = (nT)^{-1} \sum_{i=1}^{n} \sum_{t=1}^{T} \left[h(x_{it}) - K^{-1} \sum_{k=1}^{K} h(y_{itk}(b)) \right].$$

The simulated moments estimator of b is then defined as the solution to the minimization of

$$\hat{b} = \arg\min_{b} g(x, b)' \hat{W} g(x, b),$$

in which $\hat{W}$ is a positive definite matrix that converges in probability to a deterministic positive definite matrix W.

Our weight matrix, $\hat{W}$, differs from that given in Ingram and Lee (1991). First, we calculate it using the influence function approach in Erickson and Whited (2002). Second, it is not the optimal weight matrix, and we justify this choice as follows. First, because our model is of an individual firm, we want the influence functions to reflect within-firm variation. Because our data contain a great deal of heterogeneity, we therefore demean each of our variables at the firm level and then calculate the influence functions for each moment using the demeaned data. We then covary the influence functions (summing over both i and t) to obtain an estimate of the covariance matrix of the moments. The estimated weight matrix, $\hat{W}$, is the inverse of this covariance matrix. Note that the weight matrix does not depend on the parameter vector, b.

Two details regarding this issue are important. First, neither the influence functions for the autocorrelation coefficients nor the coefficients themselves are calculated using demeaned data because we obtain them using the double-differencing estimator in Han and Phillips (2010). Thus, we remove heterogeneity by differencing rather than by demeaning. Second, although we cannot use firm-demeaned data to calculate the means in the moment vector, we do use demeaned data to calculate the influence functions for these moments. Otherwise, the influence functions for the means would reflect primarily cross sectional variation, whereas the influence functions for the rest of the moments would reflect within-firm variation. In this case, the estimation would put the least weight on the mean moments, which does not appear to be a sensible economic objective.

The above described weight matrix does achieve our goal of reflecting within-firm variation. However, it does not account for any temporal dependence in the data. We therefore calculate our standard errors using the optimal weight matrix, which is the inverse of a clustered moment covariance matrix. We calculate the estimate of this covariance matrix, denoted $\hat{\Omega}$, as follows. Let ϕ_{it} be the influence function of the moment vector $g(x_{it}, b)$ for firm i at time t. ϕ_{it} then has dimension H. Note that this influence function is of the actual moment vector $g(x_{it}, b)$, which implies that we do not use demeaned data to calculate the influence functions for the means or autocorrelation coefficients, but that we do use demeaned data to calculate the rest of the moments. The estimate of Ω is

$$\frac{1}{nT} \sum_{i=1}^{n} \left(\sum_{t=1}^{T} \phi_{it} \right) \left(\sum_{t=1}^{T} \phi_{it} \right)'$$

Note that this estimate does not depend on b. Note also that if we were to use demeaned data, the elements corresponding to the mean moments would be zero.

The standard errors are then given by the usual GMM formula, adjusted for simulation error. Letting $G \equiv \partial g(x_{it}, b)/\partial b$, the asymptotic distribution of b is

$$\operatorname{avar}(\hat{b}) \equiv \left(1 + \frac{1}{K}\right) [GWG']^{-1} [GW\Omega WG'] [GWG']^{-1}.$$

Table 2: SIMULATED MOMENTS ESTIMATION

Calculations are based on a sample of nonfinancial firms from the annual 2011 COMPUSTAT industrial files. The sample period is from 1987 to 2010. The sample is split into four groups: large and small firms in the first part of the sample (through 2003), and large and small firms in the second part of the sample. The estimation is done with SMM, which determines structural model parameters by matching the moments from a simulated panel of firms to the corresponding moments from the data. Panel A reports the simulated and actual moments and the clustered t-statistics for the differences between the corresponding moments. Panel B reports the estimated structural parameters, with clustered standard errors in parentheses. λ is the cost of adjusting the capital stock, and δ is the rate of capital depreciation. μ is the drift of the profitability process, ρ_z is its serial correlation, and σ_z is the standard deviation of the innovation to this process. ρ_ψ and σ_ψ are the serial correlation of the misvaluation process and the standard deviation of its innovation. $\rho_{z\psi}$ governs the serial correlation of the two processes. ν_i and ν_r are penalties on equity issuance and repurchases. a_1 is the fixed equity issuance cost, and ϕ is the proportional debt issuance cost.

A. Moments

	Early/Small			Early/Large			Late/Small			Late/Large		
	Actual	Model	t-stat	Actual	Model	t-stat	Actual	Model	t-stat	Actual	Model	t-stat
Average net cash	-0.103	-0.134	2.537	-0.180	-0.201	1.277	0.009	-0.010	1.442	-0.134	-0.146	2.892
Std. dev. of net cash	0.142	0.201	-14.610	0.113	0.148	-9.305	0.128	0.181	-19.492	0.103	0.124	-18.968
Serial correlation net cash	0.815	0.967	-1.154	0.756	0.971	-1.296	0.887	0.957	-0.505	0.772	0.973	-1.310
Average investment	0.078	0.069	5.346	0.079	0.073	3.395	0.055	0.051	5.348	0.057	0.055	1.316
Std. dev. of investment	0.046	0.044	2.921	0.039	0.030	6.058	0.033	0.029	4.788	0.027	0.022	6.361
Serial correlation investment	0.606	0.530	0.791	0.697	0.507	1.155	0.654	0.555	2.378	0.609	0.495	0.649
Average profits	0.141	0.140	0.316	0.170	0.162	1.651	0.114	0.117	-0.641	0.153	0.150	1.513
Std. dev. of profits	0.071	0.076	-4.361	0.059	0.064	-1.540	0.062	0.067	-4.205	0.051	0.057	-3.260
Serial correlation profits	0.725	0.488	2.025	0.759	0.502	1.774	0.797	0.313	4.009	0.741	0.623	0.766
Std. dev. of Tobin's q	0.529	0.663	-6.626	0.526	0.595	-1.853	0.538	0.689	-8.928	0.434	0.504	-6.212
Serial correlation Tobin's q	0.669	0.817	-0.951	0.738	0.823	-0.567	0.642	0.780	-1.132	0.745	0.773	-0.180
Return std. dev.	0.507	0.528	-2.171	0.417	0.444	-2.910	0.547	0.526	2.657	0.440	0.415	2.492
Return serial correlation	-0.055	-0.001	-0.666	-0.069	0.005	-0.796	-0.043	-0.037	-0.082	-0.103	-0.068	-0.438
Average equity issuance	0.008	0.010	-0.769	0.006	0.004	1.344	0.009	0.008	0.783	0.005	0.005	-0.081
Std. dev. of issuance	0.031	0.037	-2.512	0.025	0.023	0.930	0.030	0.032	-0.727	0.021	0.022	-0.525
Average repurchases	0.005	0.013	-6.560	0.011	0.018	-7.000	0.005	0.016	-7.987	0.017	0.026	-3.867
Std. dev. of repurchases	0.023	0.011	3.458	0.027	0.015	3.377	0.026	0.014	3.598	0.031	0.025	11.101
Issuance-return sensitivity	0.009	0.010	-0.088	0.008	0.006	0.614	0.009	0.008	0.215	0.007	0.006	0.241
Issuance Incidence	0.062	0.092	-2.851	0.055	0.037	1.909	0.066	0.069	-0.167	0.040	0.047	-0.944

B. Parameter estimates

	λ	δ	ρ_ψ	σ_ψ	μ	ρ_z	σ_z	ν_i	ν_r	$\rho_{z\psi}$	a_0	ϕ
Early Small	1.612	0.112	0.822	0.489	-1.029	0.510	0.438	23.912	29.883	0.403	0.020	0.018
	(0.660)	(0.015)	(0.036)	(0.052)	(0.056)	(0.027)	(0.039)	(3.310)	(8.314)	(0.156)	(0.011)	(0.028)
Early Large	2.413	0.122	0.821	0.433	-0.927	0.510	0.325	29.629	19.704	0.497	0.019	0.022
	(1.712)	(0.016)	(0.042)	(0.088)	(0.136)	(0.065)	(0.040)	(10.504)	(5.377)	(0.182)	(0.005)	(0.039)
Late Small	1.893	0.111	0.778	0.455	-1.514	0.337	0.500	23.887	20.733	0.384	0.019	0.029
	(0.833)	(0.015)	(0.034)	(0.025)	(0.103)	(0.053)	(0.044)	(2.555)	(3.690)	(0.081)	(0.067)	(0.052)
Late Large	3.680	0.126	0.757	0.400	-0.724	0.631	0.281	22.795	10.118	0.333	0.017	0.012
	(2.531)	(0.029)	(0.180)	(0.080)	(0.028)	(0.019)	(0.025)	(5.492)	(2.569)	(0.591)	(0.080)	(0.046)

Table 3: SIMULATED MOMENTS ESTIMATION: PRICING KERNEL MODEL

Calculations are based on a sample of nonfinancial firms from the annual 2011 COMPUSTAT industrial files. The sample period is from 1987 to 2010. The sample is split into four groups: large and small firms in the first part of the sample (through 2003), and large and small firms in the second part of the sample. The estimation is done with SMM, which determines structural model parameters by matching the moments from a simulated panel of firms to the corresponding moments from the data. Panel A reports the simulated and actual moments and the clustered t-statistics for the differences between the corresponding moments. Panel B reports the estimated structural parameters, with clustered standard errors in parentheses. λ is the cost of adjusting the capital stock, and δ is the rate of capital depreciation. μ is the drift of the profitability process, ρ_z is its serial correlation, and σ_z is the standard deviation of the innovation to this process. ρ_ψ and σ_ψ are the serial correlation of the misvaluation process and the standard deviation of its innovation. $\rho_{z\psi}$ governs the serial correlation of the two processes. ν_i and ν_r are penalties on equity issuance and repurchases. a_1 is the fixed equity issuance cost, and ϕ is the proportional debt issuance cost.

A. Moments

	Early/Small			Early/Large			Late/Small			Late/Large		
	Actual	Model	t-stat	Actual	Model	t-stat	Actual	Model	t-stat	Actual	Model	t-stat
Average net cash	-0.103	-0.153	4.387	-0.180	-0.204	1.072	0.009	-0.010	1.090	-0.134	-0.176	3.229
Std. dev. of net cash	0.142	0.180	-9.651	0.113	0.145	-5.483	0.128	0.152	-8.009	0.103	0.148	-14.848
Serial correlation net cash	0.815	0.966	-1.154	0.756	0.962	-1.337	0.887	0.959	-0.581	0.772	0.953	-1.448
Average investment	0.078	0.074	0.654	0.079	0.074	1.058	0.055	0.046	4.154	0.057	0.046	4.868
Std. dev. of investment	0.046	0.003	4.772	0.039	0.026	3.206	0.033	0.025	6.552	0.027	0.028	-0.597
Serial correlation investment	0.606	0.224	15.689	0.697	0.534	1.032	0.654	0.645	0.058	0.609	0.553	0.313
Average profits	0.141	0.139	0.225	0.170	0.163	0.983	0.114	0.106	0.756	0.153	0.134	3.511
Std. dev. of profits	0.071	0.076	-2.804	0.059	0.069	-3.451	0.062	0.072	-6.440	0.051	0.076	-19.313
Serial correlation profits	0.725	0.731	-0.047	0.759	0.340	4.745	0.797	0.728	0.538	0.741	0.370	2.531
Std. dev. of Tobin's q	0.529	0.579	-2.208	0.526	0.578	-1.301	0.538	0.594	-2.599	0.434	0.638	-15.513
Serial correlation Tobin's q	0.669	0.497	1.731	0.738	0.834	-0.551	0.642	0.912	-2.151	0.745	0.830	-0.646
Return std. dev.	0.507	0.546	-4.307	0.417	0.426	-0.718	0.547	0.607	-6.631	0.440	0.477	-4.676
Return serial correlation	-0.055	-0.319	3.505	-0.069	0.008	-0.882	-0.043	0.044	-2.539	-0.103	0.018	-1.780
Average equity issuance	0.008	0.009	-0.596	0.006	0.006	0.568	0.009	0.010	-0.533	0.005	0.006	-1.680
Std. dev. of issuance	0.031	0.035	-2.849	0.025	0.024	0.847	0.030	0.033	-2.242	0.021	0.027	-3.002
Average repurchases	0.005	0.005	0.002	0.011	0.014	-1.601	0.005	0.017	-4.579	0.017	0.022	-2.150
Std. dev. of repurchases	0.023	0.006	3.885	0.027	0.011	3.535	0.026	0.011	3.805	0.031	0.020	6.688
Issuance-return sensitivity	0.009	0.000	1.754	0.008	0.006	0.397	0.009	0.005	2.546	0.007	0.006	0.261
Issuance Incidence	0.062	0.072	-1.282	0.055	0.059	-0.603	0.066	0.087	-2.169	0.040	0.056	-3.208

B. Parameter estimates

	λ	δ	ρ_ψ	σ_ψ	μ	ρ_z	σ_z	ν_i	ν_r	$\rho_{z\psi}$	a_0	ϕ
Early Small	4.776	0.019	0.242	0.365	-0.509	0.757	0.334	7.468	29.845	0.059	0.029	0.040
	(1.343)	(0.000)	(0.103)	(0.022)	(0.051)	(0.020)	(0.035)	(0.710)	(13.338)	(0.054)	(0.004)	(0.035)
Early Large	3.243	0.114	0.780	0.317	-1.224	0.354	0.379	29.106	29.462	0.474	0.023	0.038
	(1.296)	(0.015)	(0.060)	(0.073)	(0.258)	(0.134)	(0.037)	(9.979)	(9.839)	(0.276)	(0.008)	(0.112)
Late Small	0.057	0.016	0.766	0.356	-0.566	0.768	0.400	8.717	29.997	0.498	0.020	0.041
	(0.288)	(0.003)	(0.027)	(0.011)	(0.042)	(0.021)	(0.023)	(1.122)	(0.371)	(0.041)	(0.006)	(0.075)
Late Large	2.795	0.042	0.742	0.334	-1.296	0.397	0.483	29.910	15.484	0.485	0.030	0.036
	(1.421)	(0.004)	(0.127)	(0.109)	(0.119)	(0.053)	(0.034)	(14.310)	(3.955)	(0.308)	(0.021)	(0.115)

Table 4: PARAMETER ESTIMATES FOR INDUSTRY ESTIMATIONS

Calculations are based on a sample of nonfinancial firms from the annual 2011 COMPUSTAT industrial files. The sample period is from 1987 to 2010. The sample is split into eight industry groups. SIC13 is oil and gas extraction; SIC20 is food products; SIC28 is chemicals and allied products; SIC35 is machinery and computer equipment; SIC26 is electronic and electrical equipment; SIC38 is measuring instruments; SIC50 is wholesale trade; and SIC73 is business services. The estimation is done with SMM, which determines structural model parameters by matching the moments from a simulated panel of firms to the corresponding moments from the data. The estimation is done for each industry separately.

This table reports the estimated structural parameters, with clustered standard errors in parentheses. λ is the cost of adjusting the capital stock, and δ is the rate of capital depreciation. μ is the drift of the profitability process, ρ_z is its serial correlation, and σ_z is the standard deviation of the innovation to this process. ρ_ψ and σ_ψ are the serial correlation of the misvaluation process and the standard deviation of its innovation. $\rho_{z\psi}$ governs the serial correlation of the two processes. ν_i and ν_r are penalties on equity issuance and repurchases. a_1 is the fixed equity issuance cost, and ϕ is the proportional debt issuance cost. The bottom row of the table presents average R&D for each industry.

	SIC13	SIC 20	SIC 28	SIC 35	SIC 36	SIC 38	SIC 50	SIC 73
λ	1.583	7.085	2.797	15.691	10.377	4.439	18.971	5.534
	(0.553)	(6.882)	(2.896)	(7.876)	(14.060)	(8.191)	(25.854)	(6.113)
δ	0.118	0.092	0.115	0.053	0.056	0.117	0.037	0.118
	(0.008)	(0.032)	(0.047)	(0.020)	(0.018)	(0.088)	(0.042)	(0.031)
ρ_ψ	0.328	0.674	0.855	0.571	0.574	0.869	0.280	0.858
	(1.050)	(0.431)	(0.131)	(0.238)	(0.236)	(0.111)	(0.611)	(0.102)
σ_ψ	0.311	0.353	0.499	0.413	0.428	0.467	0.342	0.478
	(0.310)	(0.159)	(0.182)	(0.113)	(0.105)	(0.086)	(0.151)	(0.069)
μ	-1.186	-0.632	-1.041	-1.035	-0.821	-1.216	-0.742	-1.056
	(0.076)	(0.187)	(0.311)	(0.728)	(0.191)	(0.262)	(1.121)	(0.296)
ρ_z	0.342	0.673	0.502	0.544	0.657	0.423	0.694	0.497
	(0.058)	(0.062)	(0.122)	(0.304)	(0.113)	(0.124)	(0.454)	(0.141)
σ_z	0.379	0.286	0.386	0.499	0.493	0.450	0.376	0.447
	(0.107)	(0.119)	(0.130)	(0.171)	(0.076)	(0.142)	(0.286)	(0.093)
ν_i	16.713	16.296	24.533	11.454	11.585	25.510	9.694	28.170
	(20.615)	(9.770)	(10.907)	(2.776)	(3.526)	(8.864)	(5.813)	(6.588)
ν_r	28.349	7.402	29.960	8.241	10.702	29.879	5.745	28.627
	(95.226)	(5.209)	(27.695)	(2.939)	(4.352)	(22.855)	(1.810)	(15.901)
$\rho_{z\psi}$	0.327	0.343	0.343	0.260	0.301	0.458	0.282	0.485
	(1.781)	(0.941)	(0.601)	(0.427)	(0.334)	(0.223)	(0.470)	(0.188)
a_0	0.019	0.017	0.020	0.019	0.018	0.020	0.015	0.019
	(0.021)	(0.211)	(0.033)	(0.256)	(0.239)	(0.198)	(0.052)	(0.257)
ϕ	0.018	0.019	0.029	0.030	0.030	0.029	0.030	0.028
	(0.364)	(0.200)	(0.116)	(0.423)	(0.431)	(0.034)	(0.161)	(0.159)
Average R&D	0.001	0.003	0.064	0.060	0.071	0.027	0.001	0.062

Table 5: ACTUAL VERSUS MODEL IMPLIED TIME-SERIES CORRELATIONS

The figures presented are the simple correlations between annual real ex-dividend equity returns and the indicated variables. Data calculations are based on a sample of nonfinancial firms from the annual 2011 COMPUSTAT industrial files. The sample period is from 1987 to 2010. Net Saving, investment, dividends, equity Issuance, and repurchases'are all scaled by total book assets. Each variable is aggregated by taking the average across all firms in the sample in each year. The indicated correlations are then time-series correlations of these aggregated variables. Simulated calculations are based on data simulated from the model. The model parameterizations are from the estimates in Table 2.

	Early/Small		Early/Large		Late/Small		Late/Large	
	Actual	Simulated	Actual	Simulated	Actual	Simulated	Actual	Simulated
Investment	-0.286	-0.091	-0.124	-0.132	-0.605	-0.219	-0.607	-0.160
Net Saving	0.524	0.349	0.121	0.148	0.914	0.313	0.651	0.356
Equity Issuance	0.383	0.142	0.028	0.115	0.116	0.174	0.033	0.171
Repurchases	-0.400	-0.279	-0.081	-0.280	-0.801	-0.311	-0.407	-0.328
Dividends	-0.262	0.313	-0.050	0.280	-0.156	0.347	0.484	0.292

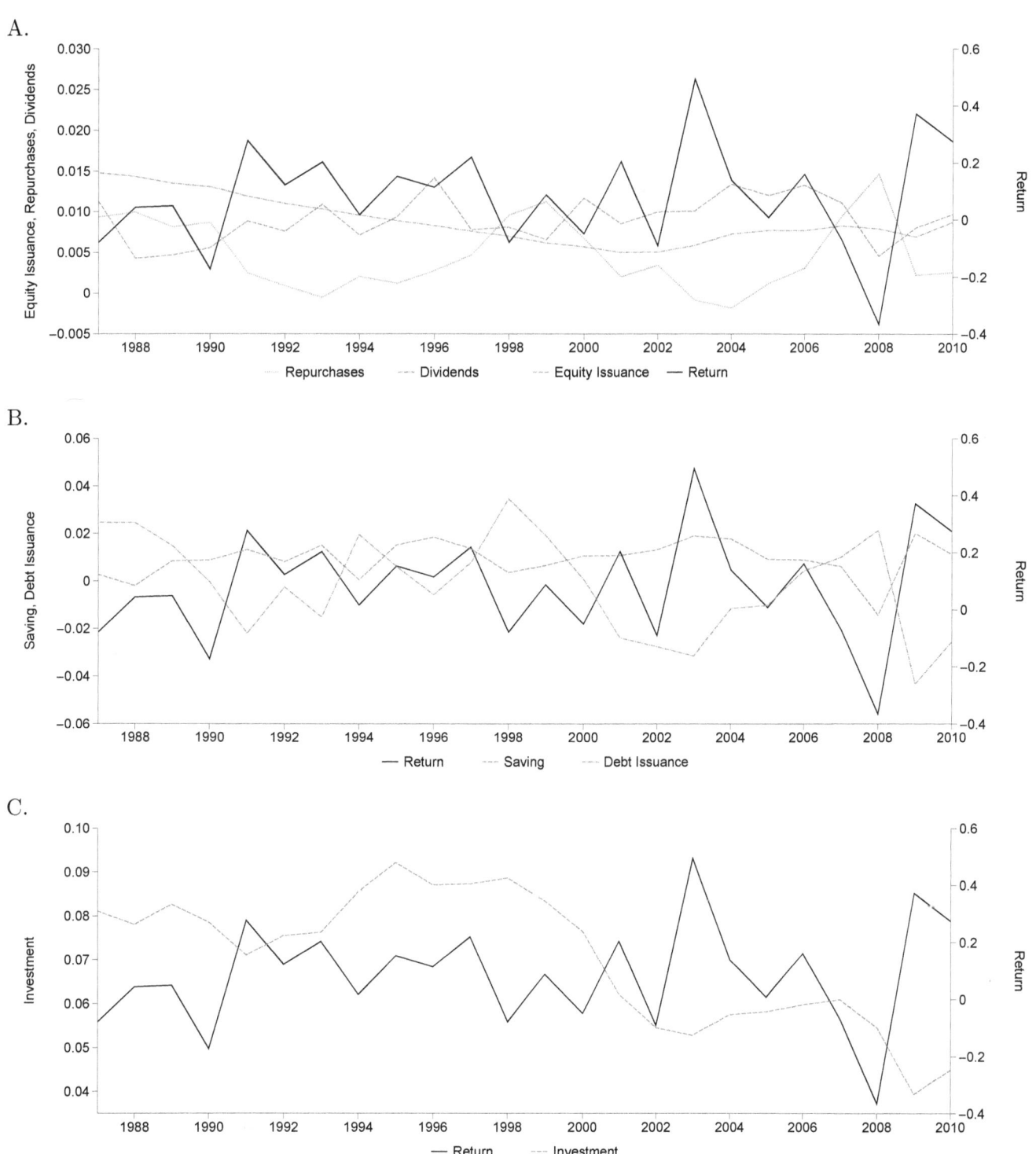

Figure 1: Time Series Patterns: Small Firms

Calculations are based on a sample of nonfinancial firms from the annual 2011 COMPUSTAT industrial files. The sample period is from 1987 to 2010. Each series is the year-by-year asset-weighted average of a particular variable. Small firms are those whose assets are below the median for a particular year in the sample. Investment, dividends, equity Issuance, saving, debt Issuance, and repurchases are all scaled by total book assets. Saving is the change in the stock of cash. Return is the real annual ex-dividend equity return.

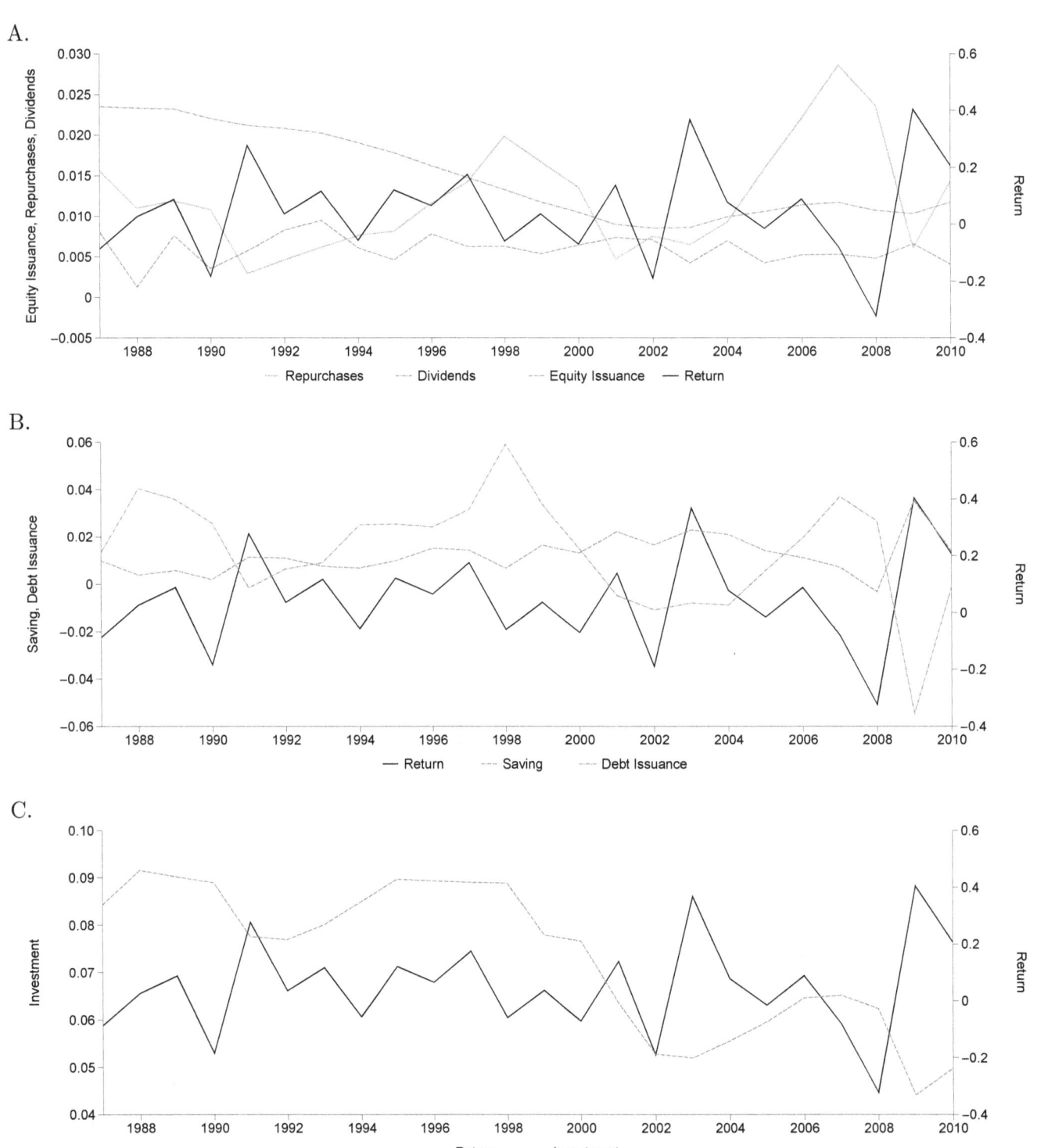

Figure 2: Time Series Patterns: Large Firms

Calculations are based on a sample of nonfinancial firms from the annual 2011 COMPUSTAT industrial files. The sample period is from 1987 to 2010. Each series is the year-by-year asset-weighted average of a particular variable. Large firms are those whose assets are above the median for a particular year in the sample. Investment, dividends, equity Issuance, saving, debt Issuance, and repurchases are all scaled by total book assets. Saving is the change in the stock of cash. Return is the real annual ex-dividend equity return.

Figure 3: Policy Functions

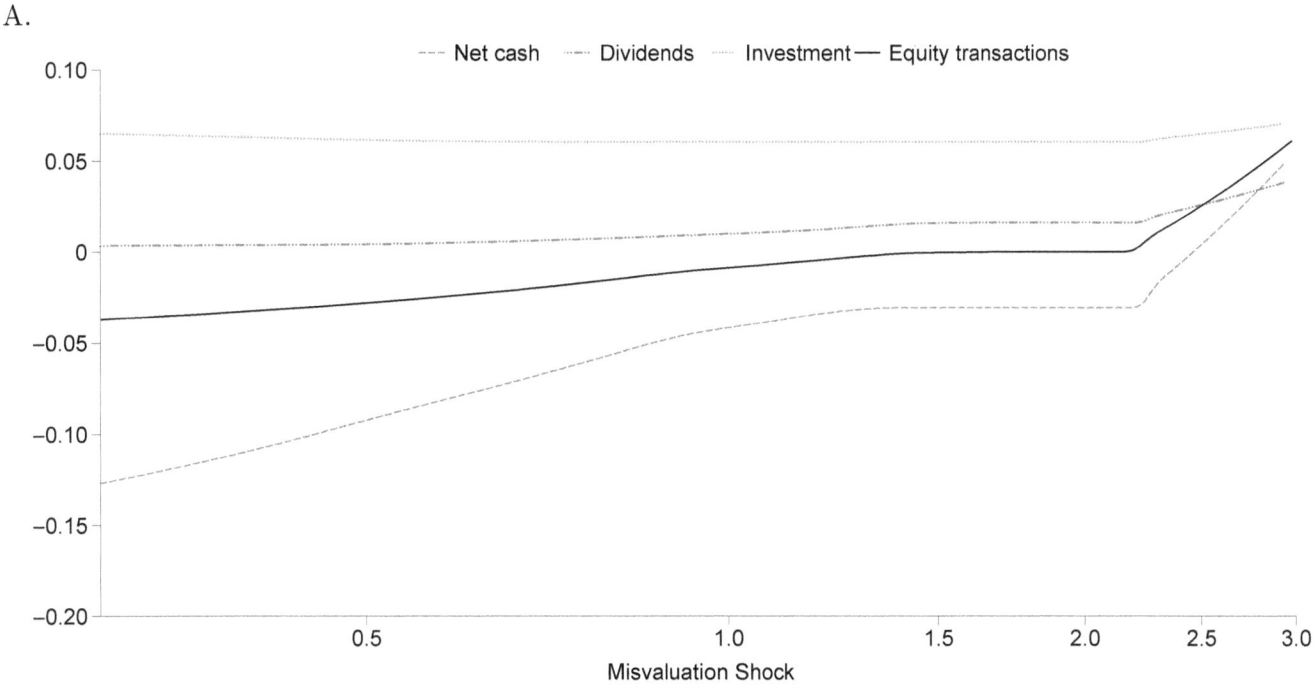

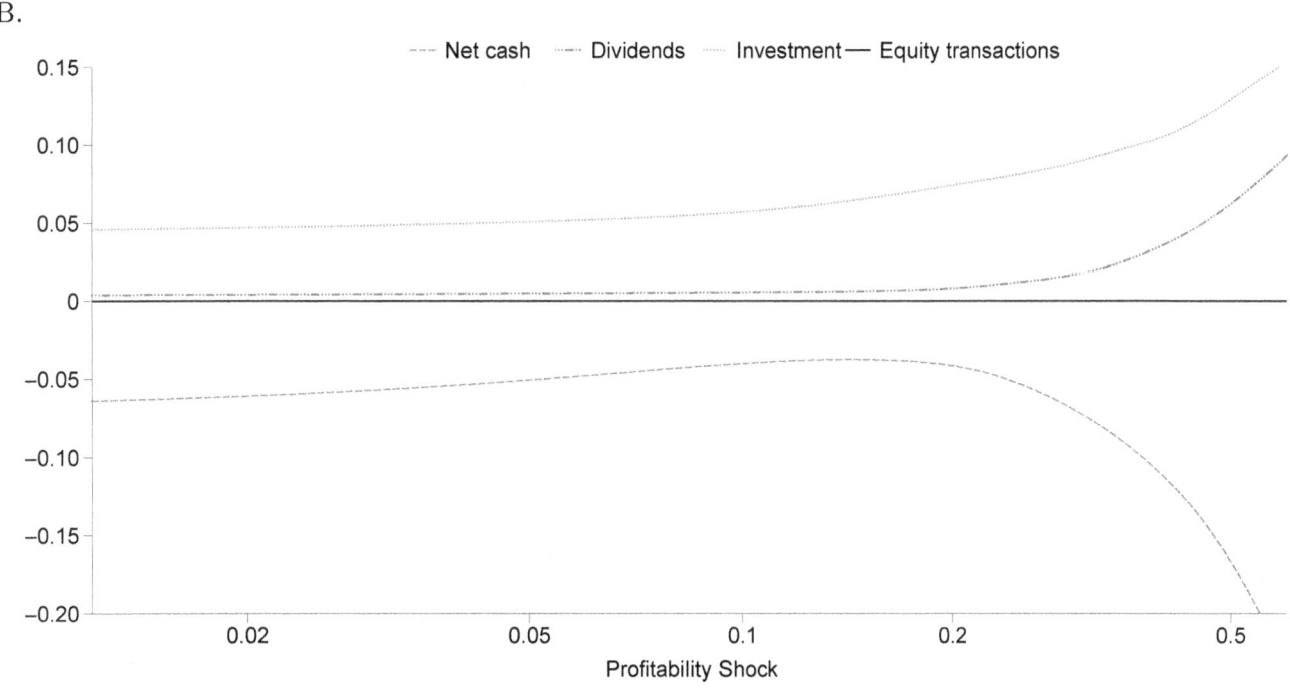

This figure depicts the optimal levels of investment, equity transactions, cash, and dividends as a function of the misvaluation shock, ψ in Panel A, and to the productivity shock, z, in Panel B. Both horizontal axes are log scale. Positive equity transactions are issuances, and negative equity transactions are repurchases. All variables are scaled by the capital stock, K.

Figure 4: Matching Moments by Industry

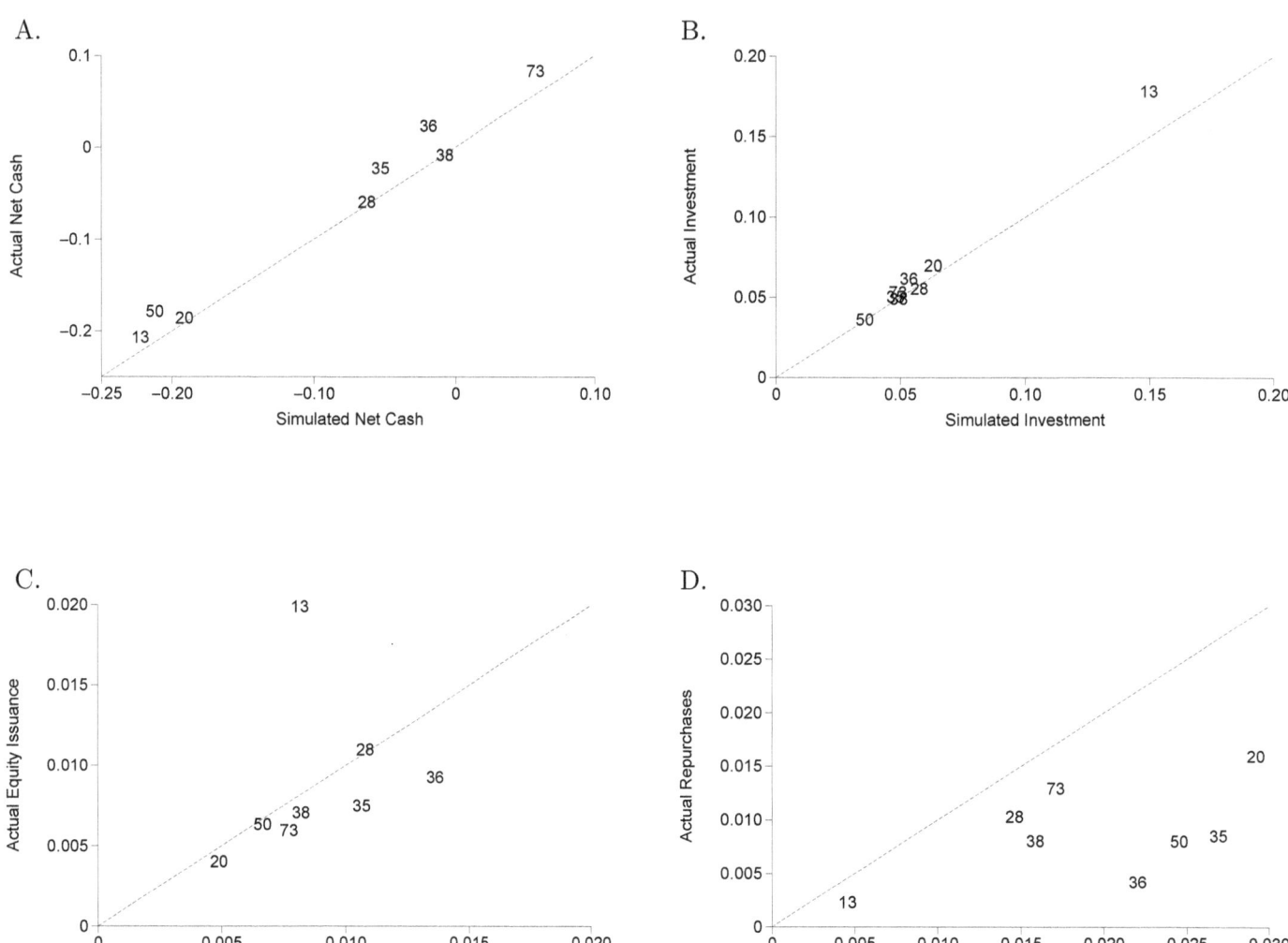

Calculations are based on a sample of nonfinancial firms from the annual 2011 COMPUSTAT industrial files. The sample period is from 1987 to 2010. The sample is split into eight industry groups. SIC13 is oil and gas extraction; SIC20 is food products; SIC28 is chemicals and allied products; SIC35 is machinery and computer equipment; SIC26 is electronic and electrical equipment; SIC38 is measuring instruments; SIC50 is wholesale trade; and SIC73 is business services. The estimation is done with SMM, which determines structural model parameters by matching the moments from a simulated panel of firms to the corresponding moments from the data. This figure plots data moments versus simulated moments for the six "mean" moments.

Figure 5: Counterfactuals

A.

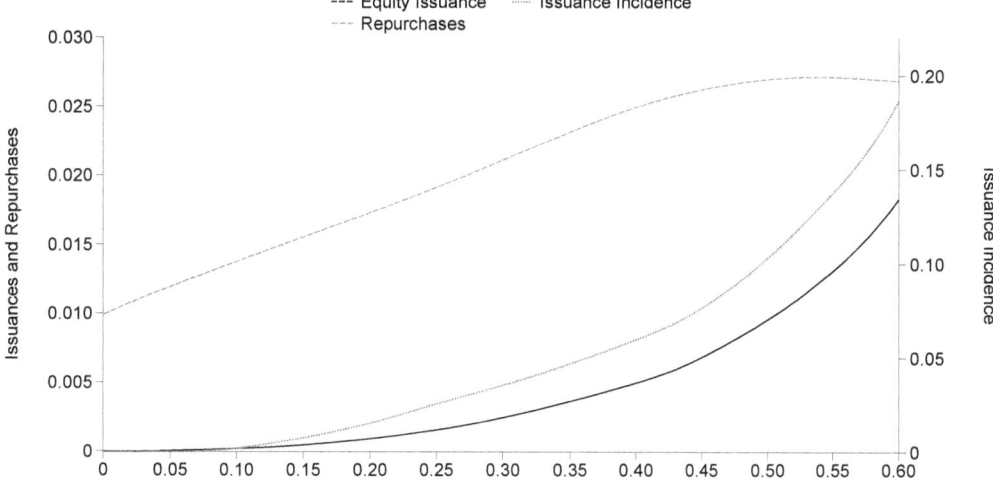

B.

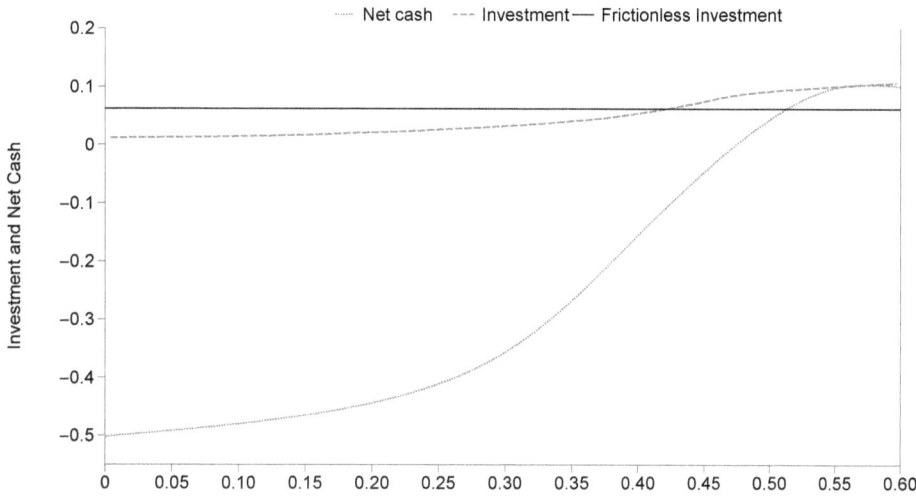

C.

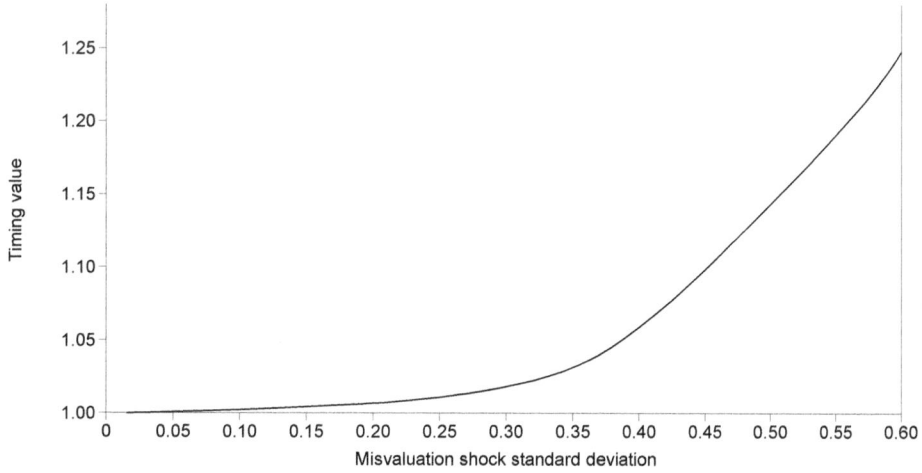

This figure is constructed as follows. We pick a grid for σ_ψ, the standard deviation of the innovation to the misvaluation shock. We then solve the model for each of the different parameter values, and then plot net cash, investment, equity issuance, equity repurchases, market value, and intrinsic value σ_ψ. Frictionless Investment is the average rate of investment from a frictionless neoclassical q model that is technologically identical to our model.

Figure 6: Impulse Response Functions

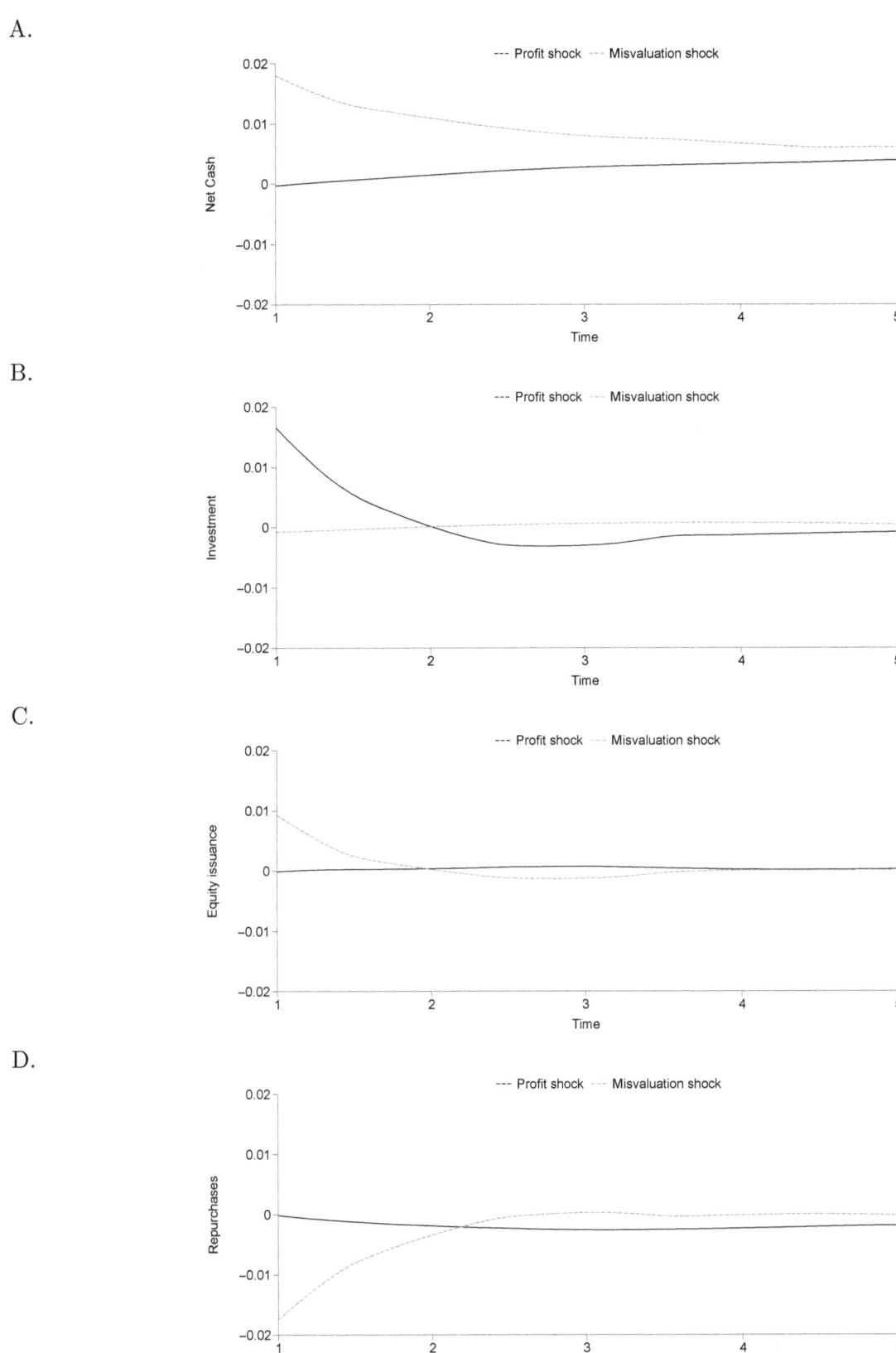

This figure depicts the responses of various variables to a one standard deviation innovation to each of the misvaluation and profit shock processes.

www.ingramcontent.com/pod-product-compliance
Lightning Source LLC
Chambersburg PA
CBHW081907170526
45167CB00007B/3182